Additional Praise for
WRITING IS MY DRINK

"For those feeling overwhelmed or battered by writer's block or self-doubt, this book is a magic carpet ride out of that muck and into wide-open, soul-connected creative flow, uncannily engaging for people who generally can't abide writing guides. And Nestor is a quietly captivating, intimate, healing storyteller—the best and rarest kind."

—Candace Walsh, author of *Licking the Spoon: A Memoir of Food, Family, and Identity*

"This is a book to savor, each delicious and thoroughly entertaining chapter revealing not just more of Theo's brilliance, but your own as well. For all those yearning to discover your own creative and unique inner literary genius, look no further. You've come home."

—Katherine Woodward Thomas, bestselling author of *Calling In "The One"*

Praise for
HOW TO SLEEP ALONE IN A KING-SIZE BED:
A MEMOIR OF STARTING OVER

"Nestor has a big heart, a real feeling for the pain and craziness of human life."

—Frank McCourt, Pulitzer Prize–winning author of *Angela's Ashes*

"Theo Nestor has an uncommon ability to evoke common yet very intense emotions. *How to Sleep Alone in a King-Size Bed* is smart, astringent, funny, precise, candid, and possesses not an ounce of self-pity."

—David Shields, *New York Times* bestselling author of *The Thing About Life Is That One Day You'll Be Dead*

"Heartbreakingly honest, wryly funny, and revelatory . . . [Nestor's] clever and relatable prose makes her tale endearing and insightful, and she sidesteps the clichés of a woman wounded with bittersweet honesty."

—LadiesHomeJournal.com

"A divorced mother's funny, chatty, revealing take on Splitsville—with just enough anguish and sadness to be utterly believable . . . An unexpected treat here is a vivid portrait of the author's thrice-married, utterly nonmaternal but generous mother . . . Women going through the pain and turmoil of separation and divorce will appreciate Nestor's candor and wit. Not another slick how-to, but a comforting reminder that life goes on after the spouse is gone."

—*Kirkus Reviews*

"Nestor writes with a self-possession and gentleness that is arresting—offering sentiment, without sentimentality."

—*Seattle Magazine*

Also by the author

How to Sleep Alone in a King-Size Bed:
A Memoir of Starting Over

WRITING IS MY DRINK

A Writer's Story of
Finding Her Voice
(and a Guide to How
You Can Too)

THEO PAULINE NESTOR

Simon & Schuster Paperbacks

New York   London   Toronto   Sydney   New Delhi

Simon & Schuster Paperbacks
A Division of Simon & Schuster, Inc.
1230 Avenue of the Americas
New York, NY 10020

First Simon & Schuster trade paperback edition November 2013

SIMON & SCHUSTER PAPERBACKS and colophon are registered
trademarks of Simon & Schuster, Inc.

For information about special discounts for bulk purchases, please contact
Simon & Schuster Special Sales at 1-866-506-1949 or
business@simonandschuster.com.

The Simon & Schuster Speakers Bureau can bring authors to your live event. For
more information or to book an event contact the Simon & Schuster Speakers
Bureau at 1-866-248-3049 or visit our website at www.simonspeakers.com.

Designed by Aline C. Pace

Manufactured in the United States of America

10 9 8 7 6 5 4 3 2 1

Library of Congress Cataloging-in-Publication Data
Nestor, Theo Pauline.
Writing is my drink : a writer's story of finding her voice
(and a guide to how you can too) / Theo Pauline Nestor. —
First Simon & Schuster trade paperback edition.
pages cm
1. Nestor, Theo Pauline. 2. Authorship—Psychological aspects.
3. Autobiography—Authorship. 4. Creation (Literary, artistic, etc.)—
Psychological aspects. I. Title.
PN171.P83N47 2013
808.02019—dc23   2013024070
[B]

ISBN 978-1-4516-6509-3
ISBN 978-1-4516-6510-9 (ebook)

For my daughters

Contents

CONTENTS

Part III: Return

Sometimes you have to play a long time to be able to play like yourself.

—Miles Davis

WRITING

IS

MY

DRINK

Introduction

Two competing forces have dominated my life: a great need to please others and an equally powerful desire for expression, a tumbleweed that has grown in mass and velocity with the passing years. Now that I'm a writer and a writing teacher, I can safely say that expression will prevail, but the imprint of the small girl who tried to make herself smaller still shimmers within me, reminding me of the long way I've come to find my own voice and to trust it.

When I was seven, my mother and I attended a horse show in which a family we knew had a couple of horses. The Wilsons were a family of accomplished children and prizewinning horses, a family together enough to obtain quilted covers for their blender and toaster. They provided a vivid contrast to my single-mom family with siblings scattered. My mother never said, "I need their approval," but even as a kid I could feel it—in her eagerness to speak, her laugh, her carefully applied pink lipstick.

After the show, horses promenaded between track and stables. I remember the satiny ribbons of blue and red and white. I loved the order of it: first place, second place, third. It was a hot California day in the mid-1960s, the hills parched yellow except for the dark green spots where old oaks offered circles of shade. I stood between my mother and one of the Wilsons' horses, taking in the all-knowing horse eye, its crazy straight eyelashes, the fly on the nose tolerated for only a second. And then the horse shuffled its hooves a bit and one hoof pressed silently onto my foot. Pain shot through me. I wanted to scream, but my mother was talking to Mrs. Wilson, and I'd been taught never to interrupt. Good manners were integral to my identity; more than once, I'd imagined a chance to curtsy—usually a fluke meeting with a queen or a Kennedy. My mother was talking very quickly, and there didn't even seem to be a quick inhale of breath in which I could wedge my voice. Finally, the pain was intolerable, and I spoke—very quietly—the line that would soon become legend: "Excuse me, the horse is on my foot."

A moment later the horse was shooed off my foot and the incident was over, but the story of my passivity lived on and has been retold so many times that it has become an emblem of my childhood self—a sort of calling card for the younger me, the timid girl too afraid to speak up when needed, or to risk the displeasure of others even at the cost of her own welfare. I cringe during the retelling of this story, which my mother tells without malicious intent and with great affection. When she gets to the

"Excuse me" part she uses the smallest of voices, unaware that my silence had once been a boilerplate item in the unspoken contract between us.

I don't mind telling this story today, though, because I now am telling it in my own voice. It's not a funny story when I tell it. "Excuse me" is no longer the punch line. The heat, the yellow hills, the fly, they're all mine. When I tell the story myself, in my own voice, I understand why the young me did not speak up sooner and I forgive her for it. Forgiving her has become an essential part of uncovering my own voice. My "uncovery."

Like many kids who grew up in the blue cloud of the 1960s, I spent the bulk of my childhood feeling like I had to be "good." I didn't come up with this on my own. Being good paid off. During the years when I was often told that I was a "good girl," one of my "difficult" sisters lived in a convent in Mexico and another sibling with a wild side vanished to do a stint in a school for wayward girls in the belly of Texas. In my child's mind, everything dear to me—including the love of others and my own survival—depended on being good.

What did being good look like? Besides shiny patent leather Mary Janes and Shirley Temple manners, being good often meant not talking about what was *really* happening. The argument that erupted downstairs after you were supposed to be asleep, mother's afternoon nap, the inviolability of the five p.m. happy hour—all of these single events cluster together, and the cluster has a name: alcoholism.

But if you don't have access to that name and if you don't talk or think about these things for long enough, you might find that you actually have no idea what you think. At least, that's what happened to me.

Writing has been part of my recovery from being good, silent, and in denial. All of these were so much a part of who I was that I have had to keep coming back to the page—to writing—to remind myself that I, too, possess a version of things, a take on the world. Not *the* take. *A* take. Mine. The page is where I am free at last from the isolation of unarticulated life, where expression takes the place of silence.

A long time before I wrote regularly and a very long time before I was published, I knew there was a writer inside me. Occasionally words would tumble onto the page in a rush and startle me with their rawness and vitality. Uncut gems tossed suddenly from a velvet bag, they magnetized me. More often than not, though, I was avoiding writing, or writing so rarely that I could never keep track of the thread of a piece. But in those rare moments of writing with abandon, I did recognize my own voice.

The road to finding my voice and letting it come to the page has been a long one. But I've come to understand the necessity of the journey, to see the length of the process as an understandable delay rather than a failing. I see now how the river of silence parallels the path that alcohol has coursed through my family, that courses through so many families. My experience serves as just one example of our many reasons for not trusting or even hearing our own voices. We've spent too long listening to everyone but ourselves; we're bombarded daily by input that renders us passive and receiving rather than active and expressing. We work in teams. We live in families. We keep peace and build consensus. Much of this is good and necessary and yet leaves us wanting something we often cannot name, something more.

For the last seven years, I've taught a nine-month course in memoir writing for the University of Washington's Professional & Continuing Education department, teaching new writers to claim their own take on the world and to write about their own experiences. Through this program, I've met scores of people who possess both a feverish desire to write and an equal measure of uncertainty about how to begin trusting themselves, who are afraid of asserting their point of view onto the page. They remind me of myself. For so long I was the one who was afraid, who had drawers stuffed with notebooks filled with half-finished stories. I was the one who didn't have the faith to stay the course from not knowing how a story would come together to at last knowing. Faith means writing past doubt, holding on to the knowledge that above the cloud cover the sky is blue. Infinitely and impossibly blue.

Although my class covers the essential elements of memoir writing—using dialogue, building a scene, creating a narrative arc—I'm reminded even as I'm teaching my students these skills that learning to trust your own voice, and even to *hear* it, is just as important as learning the technical skills of writing. Maybe even *more* important. A piece of writing can be well crafted and even eloquent and still ring hollow.

Teaching memoir writing, I've also learned that there are as many ways into writing as there are people longing to write.

Some burn to get memories down before they fade away; others feel compelled to share a story of a changing time in their lives. For me, the need to write grew out of all the years of not saying what I knew to be true, and sometimes not even allowing myself to think it. Denial, repression—you know, all that good stuff.

Writing Is My Drink is the story of how I've learned, and am still learning, to trust in my own voice and my advice on how you can too. I spent a long time hovering above the pool, afraid to dive into what I yearned to do: to write with abandon, to follow my thoughts on the page wherever they might take me without doubt or censure. At the end of each chapter, you'll find a set of "Try This" activities designed to take you deeper into your own discovery process. It might be a good idea to have one notebook or document folder that you designate just for this purpose. You can do these writing activities after reading each chapter or read the book all the way through and then return to the activities. There's no one right way. Find the one that works for you. Trust yourself; that's the key.

The accusation that we are self-absorbed—whether leveled by ourselves or by others—seems to be what emerging writers fear the most. By going off to "find our own voices," we must be narcissistic at best, or at worst the narcissist's less compelling cousin, the navel gazer. Yet, it's the work of many such "narcissists" that has given me the greatest solace in times of sadness and confusion. I have books with covers curled like furled leaves from the numerous times I've thumbed through them, scanning for that stray calming passage. When I find that passage, it inevitably settles me like the words of the most steadfast of friends. Almost everyone I know who wishes to write has a similar list of books to which they feel an enormous debt, books that have literally or figuratively saved our lives.

The time we take to find our voices is the time we need to prepare to give back. Finding the stories you want to tell and your voice as a writer readies you for the role of giver, to finally be the host. As the fabulous Anne Lamott has said in the equally fabulous book *Bird by Bird: Some Instructions on Writing and Life*: "It is one of the greatest feelings known to humans, the feeling of being the host, of hosting people, of being the person to whom they come for food and drink and company. This is what the writer has to offer."

This is my story of false starts, dead ends, and minor and major breakthroughs. You might see yourself in my story. While our individual stories of doubt may vary, a common thread runs through the stories of those of us who've deferred a dream too long. We've been very busy delaying that which we need and want to do. We know we're holding ourselves back, but that shame of believing we're the only ones failing ourselves so miserably just stalls us further. Yes, we know that most everyone else is out there procrastinating and checking e-mail too much, but we're sure our own self-doubt is the stuff of legends. It isn't. Our hesitation is simply an expected part of the road to writing—a rough first leg—but it's one we should push past, one we *can* push past.

I've come to believe that even if the process takes us longer than we want and even if our words are read by only a handful of readers—or only by ourselves—they are still worth our time and attention. Expression in itself is worthwhile. When we commit ourselves to the page, our lives become larger, if even just incrementally, and our sense of ourselves sharpens. We remember the value of our own lives and the lives of others. I don't know how this happens. I only know that it does.

Part 1
Departure

1

This Is What I Think. Tell Us What You Think.

We come to writing longing to express, and then we turn away because we are afraid. Expression comes with a price, and we know it. Once the jack-in-the-box of truth has sprung, it can't be stuffed back inside, even if no one else reads our words. Writing asks us to commit to our understanding of a situation, our take on our lives, our truth. Much of it might be benign and unthreatening, but eventually the story will ask us to give something of ourselves that we don't want to give. It may not be a Big, Dark Secret; it may even seem inconsequential to others, but it's a big deal to us. We feel exposed. We may be eager to write but still unprepared to commit ourselves—our This Is What I Think—to the page.

I traveled first into the more troubled regions of This Is What I Think in my sophomore year of college in Vancouver,

BC. I'd been dragged to a student newspaper meeting by Jean-Paul, one of my many closeted gay friends. In five years, they'd all be fully out of the closet, and I'd have enough out friends to host a modest-sized pride parade, but this was 1980.

Jean-Paul was always looking for the action, our road to fame as writers, and on this September day he decided we would be journalists. In his mind, after a few days working on our community college newspaper, we'd be Rosalind Russell and Cary Grant in *His Girl Friday*. So we sat through the first meeting of the year in the cramped *Capilano Courier* office, which smelled of rubber cement and Molson's-soaked carpeting, and by the end of the week I was the entertainment editor and Jean-Paul was gone.

I had no business being the entertainment editor of anything. It wasn't just that I was aesthetically an infant with my Fleetwood Mac albums and my love of Mary Tyler Moore. The main problem was that on most topics I had no opinion whatsoever, and if I did have an opinion, I was so worried what others might think of that opinion I could barely remember what my opinion was in the presence of another human. After a Police concert I was to review, I badgered my friends with the repeated question "So what did you think?" and then "Okay, why?" until I had enough material to patch together a review.

For a while I got away with this. The paper came out only every two weeks. I assigned some of the stories to a few hangers-on, who generally disappeared after a story or two. And frankly, since most of the time we were down to a steady staff of three—the two co-editors and myself—it was clear that if the editors called attention to how badly suited I was for this position, they'd be stuck writing all the entertainment pieces themselves, on top of the rest of our riveting community college news. One night—probably around two in the morning, four hours before our mocked-up pages were due at the printers—one of the editors said to me, "Hey, we still need an editorial. You write it this week."

Excuse me? I tried to play it cool: yes, of course, I *so* did this type of thing when I interned at *Rolling Stone* last summer. I ventured a few questions in as casual a tone as I could muster:

"Can it be on any topic?"

"Yes."

"How long should it be?"

"Five hundred words."

"How long do I have?"

"Forty-five minutes?"

Okay, I can write any opinion on any topic and I have forty-five minutes. Here we go! I tried to pull myself into a quiet corner where I could do the serious thinking required. There was no quiet corner. Our office was about four feet wide by twelve feet long. Springsteen's *Darkness on the Edge of Town* was perpetually droning out of a tape player on the windowsill, and all conversations were shouted across the length of the office. Let's face it, though: I could have been floating in the blue hush of outer space and my mind still would've been blank. Our editorials were usually on torrid topics such as the incremental increases in student fees, the machinations of our student government, or the occasional edict from our very staid administration. None of which, frankly, I had any interest in. This was a guilty secret, since I was sure that if I were genuinely smart and interesting and an *adult*, I would be interested in these things. I

did, of course, have interests, but it would never occur to me—
no matter how long I sat at that bleak corner table—that relationships, girl singers, the difficulty of writing an editorial when
you possess zero self-confidence, or the local poetry scene could
be worthy, maybe even inspired topics.

I'll save you the suspense: I choked. The whole thing is still so
embarrassing that three decades later my memory has dropped
a special protective veil over the scene so that I can only make
murky guesses about exactly how the whole thing went down.
I think I stumbled back to the editor about twenty-five minutes
later and sputtered out something like "Can't." He stared at me
and said, "What do you mean?" We went back and forth until
he was certain there was no editorial he could wring out of me.
He huffed, sat down at a typewriter, and pounded out a piece
about escalating tuition and Parliament's weak commitment to
students in approximately 6.5 minutes as waves of shame radi-
ated off me. I tried to earn my spot on the planet by copyediting
a mildewed review of the local symphony's season. In summa-
tion, I did not die.

I did not die because we never do die in those moments when
we come toe-to-toe with a version of ourselves that's a fraction
of the person we want to be. We just sniff a little and then quietly
do the necessary adjustments to live within the fencing of our
recalibrated limitations. The trouble this time, though, was that
I *knew* this limitation wasn't truly mine. I knew that deep down
I was a writer who wasn't afraid to say, "This is what I think." But
that writer was *really* deep down.

• • •

The writers I most adored throughout my twenties were the ones most willing to stake out new territory and not back down. They were unflinching. If someone bumped into me, I reflexively said "Sorry," but Gloria Steinem was willing to call out sexism where she saw it, even in herself. Erica Jong not only admitted that she had random sex and liked it, but described her pursuit of the "zipless fuck" with uncensored detail. Nora Ephron shared every sadly funny detail of her disintegrating marriage and her own neurosis in *Heartburn*.

Think about it: The writers we really admire and adore are the ones who are willing to take a risk and say what most wouldn't dare. When you're loving a piece of personal narrative, it's not just because the writing is lovely; it's because the writer is offering up something of herself on the page that most people aren't willing to give. She's saying that really scary stuff—about her husband, her friends, her jealousies, or her porn habit—that you need to hear. While it may seem like we get more than enough information about other people's private lives in our tabloid culture, we are still lacking the narrative of the complicated experience that pulses behind the story's facts. As memoirist Bernard Cooper has said, "A good memoir does more than dredge up secrets from the writer's past. A good memoir filters a life through resonant narrative . . ." And in that resonant narrative, we find our duplicity, our complexity, our complicity.

In an interview with Barbara DeMarco-Barrett on the *Writers on Writing* radio show, Mary Karr talks about the heaps of memoirs that are, she believes, all the same—reportage of the repetition of abuse. "I call them 'Sound Bite Memoirs,'" Karr says. "'I was a teenage sex slave' . . . They are one-note stories. They have one note. They show *one* aspect of *one* person. And they're usually kind of repetitive. You find out what the problem is in the beginning and it's the same problem kind of reiterated. 'My mother hit me on the head with a brick on Monday and then I was a sophomore in high school and my mother hit me on the head with a brick and then I was a junior and she hit me on the head with a brick. Then I got some car keys and I left and I'm better now.'" But the real story, Karr insists, is the one that most writers still aren't telling. "The problem isn't that your mother hit you on the head with a brick; the problem is that you still *love her*, that you depend on her."

I love that line: *The problem is that you still love her.*

If you're writing memoir, you will eventually be required to give some part of yourself you don't want to give. You don't have to give it, but if you don't, your story will suffer. It doesn't have to be sensational. As Karr said so eloquently, there are stories that tell every sordid detail but still do not invoke the emotional complexity that makes a story so human: the moment of regret, the agony of a choice, the fact that you *do* still love your mother. It's the place where your guard is completely down and your complicity vivid. You'll know when you're near it because you'll want to stop writing or take the story in another direction. It's the This Is What I Think you haven't dared to share before.

I wrote about family strife for years, or maybe I should say I'd been writing *around* it before I ever dared to say even a part of what I really thought. As a college freshman, I wrote a short story for my creative writing class titled (embarrassingly) "Keep the Home Fires Burning." Neither liberated by the mask of fiction nor galvanized by the boldness of the nonfiction stamp, the story hovered in the DMZ between fiction and memoir, possessing none of the winning attributes of either genre. The story was a cloaked portrayal of the tension that existed between my mother and my stepfather as revealed through a conversation between my stepfather and "the narrator" as they walked the circuit of a golf course on a dewy morning, my stepfather golfing, the narrator caddying.

In my defense, the story with its oblique themes was dimly reflective of the hills-like-white-elephants aesthetic that was very chic in the college's English department that year. But unlike in Hemingway's coded story of abortion, it was never completely clear what this great conflict was that the characters were woodenly sidestepping. Behind the smoke, there were two people on their third marriages arguing their way to the bottom of a bottle most nights, but as an eighteen-year-old I wasn't ready to see that, let alone name it and bring it to the page. The class and teacher responded with confusion. What's really going on? What are the characters talking about? "For God's sake, just come out and say it," a kid in the corner finally cried.

Many years later, as an MFA student, I felt once again defeated by a lackluster class response to another of my stories about family: Again the conflicts were muffled and the story aimless. I ran into a fellow student on my way out of the creative writing office who, after hearing my troubles, calmly suggested, "Why don't you try writing about what scares you the most?" She was writing a clearly autobiographical story of leaving her husband for a woman. Was I the only person who was afraid of being struck down by lightning? What was wrong with me?

That night I sprung out of bed at two a.m. and booted up

the computer, ready to do what I'd delayed for decades. The response to the directive Write About What Scares You the Most was unfolding frame-by-frame across the screen of my mind.

The opening scene is an early morning in January 1991. The narrator is driving across the Nevada desert toward the Grand Canyon, the place where she'd conceived a child six years earlier. As she drives toward the canyon, the stunningly yellow sun rising in her eyes, the memory of this earlier trip to the Grand Canyon comes back to her in shards. She tries to blink the memories away with the sun, but as she drives eastward, she dives deeper into the memory of the cold January of 1985. It was a snowy winter weekend at the South Rim, deep wells of snow at the base of the Ponderosa Pines, the sky a startling blue. She was twenty-three and there with a man she never should have been with, wandering the frosty white edge of the red canyon by day, drinking Scotch in the lodge by night.

There it was: the thing I didn't want to give. I was reluctant to release the story of my own abortion to the page, but mostly I wanted to keep buried the guilt I'd carried for years. But this time I wrote past the electric fence of reluctance. I'd burned up all my stalling time. I knew that if I were going to be a writer, I had to stop hiding. As I typed rapidly in the dark, sweat ran down my sides. Two hours later, I typed the last words of my first true This Is What I Think.

I lived.

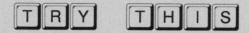

1. Think back to a time when you couldn't rise to the writing task or say what needed to be said. If you could relive that moment, what would you write or say now?

2. Make a list of writers you admire for their willingness to travel to the land of This Is What I Think.

3. List pieces of writing that have changed your life as a direct result of the risk the writer was willing to take.

4. List people you know or admire from afar who routinely share their unpopular opinions with others.

5. Post these lists near your writing space or keep a document with this list on the desktop of your computer.

6. Make a list of the topics that would scare you the most to write about. You don't have to write about these now, or ever. But you might. Keep the list in a secret place if you want. Sometimes I feel freer in making such a list if I write the items in a shorthand that reminds me of a specific and private moment ("trip to the Grand Canyon") but wouldn't mean much to anyone else.

7. Type the words "This Is What I Think" in boldface at the top of a page and print out several copies. Use these pages for ten-minute timed writings. Try not to stop and edit during these timed writings but instead just let your thoughts pour onto the page. You can write about anything you like during these writings. Hopefully, the words at the top of the page will be emboldening. I'm a big advocate for writing by hand but find what works for you.

8. Three-hole punch your This Is What I Think writings and keep them in a binder.

9. Browse through your This Is What I Think writings on occasion, looking for ideas you want to expand upon. Pick one and write for another ten minutes, diving even deeper into your idea.

10. Challenge: Watch for news stories related to your This Is What I Think. Then, write an op-ed piece for your local newspaper based on This Is What I Think. (If you do this, send me an e-mail and let me know. I'll think of it as making up for that editorial for the community college paper I should have written many moons ago.)

11. Go listen to some great author interviews on Barbara DeMarco-Barrett's radio show *Writers on Writing* at PenOn Fire.Blogspot.com.

2

Zen Buddhism for Complete Fraidy Cats

On the best days, you write with abandon, moving forward and forward and forward into you do not know what, jumping from rock to boulder, never once looking down at your feet. The line that separates writer and writing burns away like a mirage on the desert horizon. It's just go, go, go.

And then there's the rest of the time.

To paraphrase Miles Davis, it's taken a long time for me to sound like myself. If I can write with abandon at least some of the time, I'm doing well. We don't want to accept that we're only working the way we want to work *some* of the time, but the truth is it's not easy to induce a state of reckless abandon. Ditto for *willing* oneself into letting go. Acceptance holds part of the key. But for some of us, holding on tight has been the norm for a very long time.

Even as a kid, I had trouble letting go. A child insomniac, I read and ruminated by night and rested my head on cool school desks by day. I obsessed over my emergency plan for what to do if I lost my mom in the grocery store. As a child, I never had a name for this. Now I can see that anxiety runs through both sides of my family, although not everyone is ready to own that.

"No, never," my mom said with a shrug when a nurse recently asked her if she had ever had anxiety or depression.

"Oh, okay," said the nurse. "How about any *family* history of anxiety or depression?"

My mom was just about to wave that off, too, when I said, "Uh, yeah, go ahead and put me down for that."

At twenty-three, I was on the Road to Nowhere, treading water in Santa Fe, where I waited tables at a Canyon Road café, drank a lot of wine, and spent a lot of lazy mornings eating breakfast burritos and drinking coffee with the other waitresses as we all put off the effort of going for our dreams. If I could go back and interrogate this younger version of myself, I wonder if she'd crack and confess to her dream of becoming a writer. I know she looked on with awe when she refilled the coffee cup of the thirty-something woman named Natalie sitting at the corner table, writing furiously in her notebook. In a San Francisco bookstore a few years later I'd find her book, *Writing Down the Bones: Freeing the Writer Within*, a book that has since become hugely popular for the encouragement it offers writers. Maybe all that coffee I poured helped her along. I myself was miles from being able to encourage anyone to do anything productive, let alone write, the one thing I knew deep down that I did want to do. The next year I'd be going back to school to finish my undergrad degree, but for now I was a waitress whose future didn't extend past my plans for Friday night.

Then one day the Canyon Road café was bought by a student of Zen Buddhism and overnight the staff—except for myself— was replaced by a pack of Zen Buddhists who'd followed their leader from San Francisco after he'd been run out of the Zen Center there. These ZB's were mostly in their thirties and forties. Some of them wore their brown robes and wooden beads to the breakfast shift, coming straight from their meditation pillows at the Zendo, a wake of smug serenity frothing up behind them.

In theory, the teachings of Buddha seem pretty sound to me. Desire is the source of all suffering. Agreed! In theory, I could be a Buddhist. In real life there's just one thing stopping me: my entire being. Buddhism is about detaching. That's great, but my twenty-three-year-old self was all about latching on, clinging, and whimpering.

So when the Buddhists took over the restaurant and started doing their calm-faced bows after dropping the check and speaking in modulated voices in the kitchen, I felt a sudden urge to be more hostile than normal: to openly judge others, to say "Fuck it!" when I spilled (which was often), to chain-smoke on breaks, to be moved to sudden petulance by slight changes in protocol and procedure, and to whine relentlessly about the uncontrollable, such as the heat, the cold, and the verbal tics of Texan tourists.

Most of the Zen Buddhists paid no mind to my annoying behavior, but there was one person who I bugged the hell out of: my manager, Steve. How do I know this? Because one time after he posted a new schedule on which I was yet again assigned the worst shifts imaginable, I asked him what was up.

He looked me square in the eye and said evenly in a voice thick with Zen Buddhist detachment: "I don't like you."

I don't *like* you? Who *says* that?

After that the gloves were pretty much off, and Steve and I did all but ram each other with our serving trays as we passed through the dining room. We did not pretend to like each other. This didn't seem to bother him, because in his detached and spiritual state he didn't care one bit whether I liked him or not; and besides, he was the manager, so my not liking him had absolutely no bearing on his life or well-being. I, on the other hand, was cracking under the misery of such open disregard and was becoming more broke every day I worked yet another breakfast shift.

Then one day, during the exhaustion of post–Sunday Brunch chaos, Steve and I were standing at the espresso machine, chatting. For some reason Steve was trying to be friendly, perhaps because we'd together just taken on an understaffed restaurant stuffed with rich, mimosa-seeking tourists. We were talking about how he'd lived in San Francisco, where he'd studied at the Zen Center, how much he'd liked it *there*, how things were better *there*, of course.

"Actually," I said, remembering this connection for the first time, "my great-aunt was a student at the Zen Center a long time ago."

"Oh," he said, in the voice of someone who's just realized

that someone they've systemically considered to be of no interest might have something mildly interesting to say.

"Who's your aunt?"

"Pat Herreschoff."

His jaw dropped as if I'd answered, "The Dalai Lama." Finally, he said in a quiet voice that couldn't conceal how dis-
turbed he was, "That's not possible."

"What do you mean?"

"It's not possible that Pat Herreschoff is *your* aunt," he said,
his trademark contempt returning.

I knew exactly what he meant. It didn't seem possible to me
either.

The first time I was conscious of meeting my great-aunt Pat,
she was wearing long, flowing brown robes, a tangle of wooden
beads, and her head was shaved. Completely shaved. The year
was most likely 1966, a time when women wore nylons and
pumps to the grocery store. A year when the words "divorcée"
and "spinster" explained the existence of inexplicable women. A
year when the girls at my school were forbidden from wearing
pants. Two years later the moratorium on pants for girls would
be lifted, but for a long time afterwards I still wore dresses. Playing it extra safe, I guess.

When Aunt Pat walked through the door, my eyes lingered
a minute or two on her shorn head, resting upon the gray
shadow of stubble longer than any adult might allow herself.
I was five.

My reverie was broken when my grandmother, JoJo, asked, "You remember my sister, Pat, don't you?"

I was certain I'd never met this person before in my life.

"She might've been in street clothes last time," she added, as if this were a minor detail—as if all of us have "street clothes" that we occasionally trade off for a crazy brown flowing robe to be sported with no hairdo whatsoever.

Aunt Pat scared me, but in the good way—like watching fire barely contained. I knew I was in the presence of a woman who wasn't afraid to say no, who'd learned to trust herself. When that razor hits your scalp, I suppose you've pretty much made up your mind not to play nice anymore. The women in my world back then minced about in high heels and bleached their hair to a Marilyn-inspired platinum. They wore false eyelashes, thick black eyeliner, and pale lipstick. Their lives were shaped by the course of their relationships. By comparison, Aunt Pat was barely female. She lived somewhere beyond gender, and even at five I recognized this sort of noncompliance as dangerous. It seemed to me that she inhabited a world beyond approval, and I would not understand for many years that it was possible to breathe, function, and exist without a constant IV drip of approval.

We'd gone out to lunch at Bob's Big Boy near the Stanford Shopping Center in Palo Alto. A five-year-old girl in patent leather shoes, her grandmother, and a woman of a certain age with a shaved head and flowing brown robes, we sat together in the big red Naugahyde booth sipping our Shirley Temples.

"I have a present for you," Aunt Pat said, leaning across the table in that frosty air-conditioned restaurant on that hot California day in 1966. "This is one of my favorite books. I want to give you my personal copy," she said as she passed me a book across the table.

Excitedly, I examined the cover: a line drawing of a girl, her pig, and a dangling spider on the cover. I read the title on the book's clean, unbroken spine: *Charlotte's Web*.

"But you didn't read *this* copy? Did you?" I asked, holding up the book. "The spine doesn't have any cracks. It looks brand-new."

"That is the copy I read, my personal copy," she said, and her eyes met mine. I saw something powerful there that startled me, something I couldn't name at the time, but I think now I can. Her eyes were full of intention. In fact, it seemed that everything she said and everything she did was full of intention. In that moment she began to represent for me the possibility of becoming exactly who you set out to be: a Buddhist, a writer—if you wanted—or merely a magical person who could read a book without leaving any evidence that you'd passed through its pages.

In those don't-ask-don't-tell times, portraits of family members evolved slowly. To boot, Pat was a student of Zen; her skill set included deflecting, speaking in koans, and the ability to answer any question with a question without skipping a beat. But over the course of my childhood and adolescence, I collected a handful of remarkable details about Pat, the most amazing of which was that she was one of the first American women to be ordained a Zen Buddhist priest. By my early twenties, Pat loomed large in my mind. Her calm confidence made her the poster child for everything I was not.

Two years before my conversation with Steve, I'd gone to visit Aunt Pat on the North Shore of Oahu, where she lived in a tiny studio apartment attached to a low wooden house just yards away from the crazy Pacific. My boyfriend and I had spent the night in a mosquito-infested tent a few miles away because I didn't want to impose on her. We arrived after lunch on New Year's Day, 1983.

I was eager and excited to see her because I imagined she would recognize how evolved I was and I would receive some Zen master nod of approval in front of my boyfriend, Markos. No longer a little girl afraid of women who shaved their heads, I now saw Aunt Pat as a bit of a hippie girl status symbol and was excessively proud that she'd studied with Shunryu Suzuki, known to many as the author of *Zen Mind, Beginner's Mind*, at the San Francisco Zen Center. I'd imagined that she'd embrace me as a kindred spirit, as brave, independent, and self-possessed.

She took us first to see her Japanese rock garden behind the house: a series of boulders surrounded by swirling eddies of perfectly raked gravel. I tried to ooh and aah over the rocks in a manner that communicated both that I understood the beauty in the austere and understated and that I wasn't an overly talkative people pleaser. We then made our way back inside. Her tiny place was covered in tatami mats, a couple of low tables holding a teapot, some books, a couple of hand-thrown bowls. The sort of cement block and board bookshelf that every college student seemed to possess in 1979 sectioned off her sleeping area. In another corner, a cramped kitchen housed a hot plate and an early model fridge full of alfalfa sprouts and pressed tofu. Pat served us tea at her table by the giant windows that looked onto a beach of black volcanic rocks. The surf roared relentlessly; salt hung in the air.

"How about a walk?" she said after tea, rising from the little table. The three of us—my tiny aunt of barely five feet and one hundred pounds, my long-legged boyfriend, and myself—headed then toward the water. As we moved closer, I scanned the rocky beach for the sandy strip we would be walking along, but there was nothing beyond the jumble of black volcanic rocks between which the loud, violent surf surged in and out. Pat leapt to the first gnarled black outcropping and then sprung effortlessly to the next. Markos jumped behind her, not quite as quick and agile but nearly. I scrambled up the first jagged lava chunk and there I stood, frozen, arms windmilling to steady myself as waves rushed up onto the rock.

Finally, I slunk down the rock, trudged through the surf, and clambered up the next chunk of volcanic material, bent over and clinging to the rock with my hands for balance. I made slow progress this way. As the gap between Pat and Markos and myself grew, I feared the moment they would look back and then feel compelled to wait. As soon as they did, I would be separate from them; they would be together—the competent people—and I would be left alone with my inability, my anxiety waving like a flag. This moment came quickly. There I was, the most awkward creature on earth, dragging myself forward as my patient sixty-six-year-old aunt and strapping twenty-two-year-old boyfriend looked on. I felt completely revealed, the parts of myself I'd worked for so long to keep covered exposed. I could barely meet Markos's eyes. In our six months together, I'd managed to keep my giant self-doubt mostly out of view. What would he think?

I didn't make it much farther before they started heading back. Because of me, they were cutting the walk short. Ugh! They caught up with me quickly, and we walked back to my aunt's mostly in silence, the two of them leaping from rock to rock at a visibly slowed pace and me taking up the rear, my face burning with shame. When we reached the lawn between Pat's house and the beach, Markos gave me that It's-okay look intended to comfort but which never does. Pat looked at me without judgment and said evenly and not unkindly, "You just lack confidence."

Just, I thought, irritated. I knew I lacked confidence, but I wanted that to be my secret. I had no idea how I might possibly gain confidence. Lacking confidence seemed so permanent, like youth.

Besides lugging around my duffel of self-doubt, I was also saddled with the self-imposed task of keeping the whole thing under wraps. I talked with bravado some of the time and laughed loudly all of the time. I figured I could talk up enough smoke and mirrors so that no one would sense how little faith I had in myself, my feet, my body, my abilities.

Here's a short list of the things I could not do:

- leap from rock to rock above swirling surf (covered above)
- fall back into a circle of hands (This barely ever comes up, although it did once in eighth grade drama class and no, I couldn't do it.)
- ski fast (I could ski slowly.)
- rappel

- rock climb
- leap from log to log (It may not seem like a big deal, but I grew up in British Columbia, where log leaping is practically required of every adolescent. Many a teen beer party begins and ends with a stint of log leaping.)
- water-ski
- dive into cold water
- dive into warm, tropical water
- emergency rescue
- trust someone to love and take care of me
- write with abandon

Before I could let go—even just a little—I had to discover what I'd been holding on to. And sometimes we can't discover what we've been holding on to before we're utterly ready. In other words, we must be miserable.

When I was twenty-five, I moved from Santa Fe to San Francisco, where I, in fact, ended up living just blocks from that same San Francisco Zen Center where both Steve and Pat had studied. Out of loneliness I went there once to see if I could feel something—a connection to my aunt Pat (although she hadn't been there since the seventies) or maybe a great inspiration to study Zen—but I felt nothing.

During the last two years of the four years I lived in San

Francisco, I would ride my bike across the park to the Richmond District on Tuesday afternoons and sit in a therapist's office. It cost seventy dollars an hour, roughly the tips from a night of waitressing. I had a problem I couldn't name. I didn't even know where to dig to unearth the thing. After months of discussing all my everyday anxieties—over money, over relationships, over finding my way in the world—I finally touched a soft spot, the sinkhole I'd spun circles around for so long.

"Do you think your mother's an alcoholic?" my therapist asked. She was ten years older than me, with frizzy brown hair and a last name like an Italian mountain town.

An alcoholic? I thought of an expression—one of my mother's, in fact—"a falling-down drunk." My mother wasn't that. Yes, there was a glass of wine beside her in the evenings; and yes, the sound of two ice cubes hitting a glass and clicking against each other summoned up her image. Every time. But she wasn't a *drunk*.

I thought of my real father then too. He *was* an alcoholic, and I was allowed to call him that because he'd named himself that when he joined AA when I was twenty-one. I could call him that because when he drank he was loud and obnoxious. I even had a scar on my hand from where he burned me accidentally with his cigarette when I was eight. He'd been trying to what—hug me? tickle me?—when the cigarette singed my skin. I'd jumped back, and we'd both looked at each other, wary. The scar is a small circle, still here although ever so faint. I think of it as a sun, a child's perfectly round sun.

Yes, I could name him as an alcoholic easily, even casually:

32

My dad's an alcoholic. Because he'd said it himself, called it out, given it a name and a place in the world. Naming him an alcoholic involved no betrayal on my part. I could also say it because he was dead.

But my mother?

"An alcoholic? No, I don't think so," I said, eager to end the session and get out of there.

"Would you be willing to explore the idea that your mother has a problem with alcohol? That her drinking has affected your relationship with her?"

I looked out the open window, to the backs of the Victorian houses of yellow, white, and blue with their fire escapes lacing down their sides. It was a city built on disaster, on hope, on a history of buildings collapsing, a city of people needing a way out in a hurry.

"Maybe," I said, and the session was over.

But finally the day would come: the day when I would take the word "alcoholic" and my mother and put them together in a sentence. And that—that was a changing day.

In some important way, that was the day I became a writer. I say it began that day even though I had been writing sporadically in a creative way and routinely in an academic way for years. I say it began that day even though the writing I would come to think of as my "real writing" was still years down the road. I say it began that day because that was the day I jumped off the cliff and was willing to say what I really thought even if it meant the loss of everything I believed I needed to survive, even if it meant pissing people off, even if abandonment was to follow.

That was the day I let the razor hit my scalp. The day I made a first step in letting go of the idea that everybody needed to like me all the time. The day I stopped making nice for a moment and accepted that the Steves of the world might never like me, and that I would be okay.

As it turns out, I was, in fact, a grown person who didn't require the approval of my mother or anyone else to survive, but without writing, I learned, part of me would never have a chance to come to life. The story that I began to write that day was my own version of my life, the story we each have a right to tell, if only to ourselves. But it's a right we must take; no one will ever hand it to us.

Like diving into cold water, writing requires some letting go. Writing requires trust: trust that words will find you, that the unknown will become known, that the mystery will be solved, that the story will find its arc, that you will find your story and your voice, that your voice will be heard, that you will be understood. But most of all, writing requires you to trust yourself, the source of the voice inside you that supplies the next word, the next line, the next idea. And until you can access some of this trust, you won't be able to write the stories you want to write the way you want to write them.

For some of us, the road to finding our own voice is a long one, because we're not ready for the truth of the fact that the only way out is through. We don't feel ready to see ourselves reflected back to us, to sit through a million competing thoughts—the static we must often endure before we finally find the station where our own voice comes through singular and clear, before we can write with abandon on a semi-routine basis, before we can press our vision past the block, past the half-finished story, past the rewrite, until finally we arrive at a finished piece of writing that is, in fact, a manifestation of our vision and that does, in fact, tell our story the way we want to tell it. So much encouragement and faith is required to write like a child and revise like a grown-up.

But it can be found; even if you have to stumble forward in blind faith, you can start down the path. You can sit through all the bad first drafts, revisions, and doubt. You can face all the places you're sure you fall short and keep going. You can push past the doubt, the fear, and the part of you that's afraid of wanting something this much.

1. As fast as you can, make a list of times when you could not access trust in yourself. Hint: Here's what not accessing the trust looks like. You had a hunch and you didn't follow it. You knew the relationship would fail but you started in on it. Your inner voice said, "Do it," but you didn't. Your inner voice said, "Run," and you stayed. You watched TV instead of going to the party. You were ashamed. You said you "couldn't" when in fact you just "wouldn't." You passed on the free plane tickets. When you had an idea, you batted it away. When you wanted something, you told yourself it was too much to hope for. The novel in the drawer. The unmade phone call. The made bed. The unsung song. The words you didn't say. The class you didn't take. The questions that burned inside you but you wouldn't ask.

2. Write for five minutes without stopping about one of these times.

3. As fast as you can, make a list of times when you were able to access trust. You wrote without thinking. You skied fast. You dove in. You didn't stop to feel guilty. You bought the art supplies. You followed the hunch.

4. Write for five minutes about one of these times.

5. Pick two more times—one from each list. Write about them together.

6. Make a list of the people who've helped you to trust in yourself.

7. Post this list near your writing desk.

8. When you get scared, look at the list.

3

How I Got Through My Worst Block Ever

(and How You Can Too)

Before Mary Karr's *The Liars' Club* and Frank McCourt's *Angela's Ashes* ushered in the memoir craze that ignited in the mid-1990s, only a few lone-wolf memoirs could be spotted on the horizon: Maya Angelou's *I Know Why the Caged Bird Sings*; Maxine Hong Kingston's *The Woman Warrior*; Russell Baker's *Growing Up*; Tobias Wolff's *This Boy's Life*; arguably even James Baldwin's *Notes of a Native Son*. The civil rights, gay rights, and women's rights movements of the 1960s fostered our sense of the importance of the individual's story of awakening. The early seventies gave rise to the New Journalism, a quirky first-person nonfiction that lived in the no-man's-land between journalism and memoir (Hunter S. Thompson's *Fear and Loathing in Las Vegas*, Joan Didion's *Slouching Towards Bethlehem*). The literary conditions that would herald in new bookstore shelves labeled "Memoir" were falling into place, but for the most part, rabid fans of first-person realism like myself depended upon the autobiographical novel, such as Sylvia Plath's *The Bell Jar*, Jack Kerouac's *On the Road*, Erica Jong's *Fear of Flying*, and Nora Ephron's *Heartburn*.

Aside from those few important exceptions, we didn't have the possibility of memoir as a genre in the eighties, the time when I first dreamed of becoming a writer. It was a dark time. Duran Duran dark. We didn't have memoir, but we did have the Brat Pack. We had *Less Than Zero*; we had *Bright Lights, Big City*. And we had Tama Janowitz and her damn *Slaves of New York*. These writers were writing a sort of *cinéma vérité* fiction, fiction that read like memoir, but memoirs of a particular class and place, memoirs of everything that I was not.

These books sprung from the self-referential impulse of moneyed, big-city youth—in New York or LA, usually—a few years out of the Ivy League. The main characters possessed plenty of resources, breeding, and powerhouse networking connections to fall back on when the coke ran out. And they were male, except for Janowitz. So it was Janowitz who became the focus of my first case of writer envy. Like me, she was female and writing about "real" stuff. Unlike me, she had oodles of long hair and a tiny waist, and lived a groovy Lower East Side life that people actually wanted to read about.

I loved *Slaves of New York* and I hated it. I hated it because my life was so impossibly off-center. I spent my coming-of-age years in Canada, not New York. I went to a community college, not Yale, and at the time *Slaves* hit the bookstores, I was living in the middle of the desert, waiting tables in a Cajun restaurant. I was twenty-five and just about to receive the college degree I should have received three years earlier if I hadn't dropped out to travel, party, make batik T-shirts, waitress, and drink coffee by day and vodka cranberries by night with other aimless youth. In between all that, I read a lot. Although I possessed an amorphous desire to be something called a *writer*, I didn't know what I wanted to write. I knew no writers. I had no idea where to begin the career trajectory that goes from waitress to writer.

But like almost every other time when I've needed to figure out the way, a friend came along with an idea to get me headed in the right direction. One of my fellow waitresses, Sara, had won a writing contest when she was a senior at Barnard the year before. Like every other waitress I knew, she was a ball of potential genius that orbited around the streets of Santa Fe without purpose; we were all on hold together, waiting for our miracles. I read Sara's prizewinning short story—full of gritty East Coast realism and disenfranchised youth, very pre-memoir in the tradition of Bret Easton Ellis and the gang—and got inspired. I'm pretty sure it was Sara who suggested I consider applying to MFA programs, so I semi-randomly picked one—UC Davis—and set my sights on it. It probably wasn't the wisest decision to apply to just one school, and for that school to be in the middle of a farming valley where I knew exactly no one, but from what I can remember, my distorted thought process looked like this: (1) even though I never finish anything I write, I will get into any school to which I apply, and (2) UC Davis is vaguely near San Francisco, which is where I'd really love to live if I had the courage.

So the application process began. First up: the GRE. Let's

just say, apparently you *do* need to study for it—that's real—and if you're taking the subject test as well as the maddening general test, you might want to bring a lunch, as you'll be at the industrial wasteland testing site for eight hours, and without a lunch you'll almost be hallucinating around two p.m. when you're deciding between darkening the bubble beside the name "John Milton" or the one beside "Jonathan Swift." The general test was 3.5 hours of questions like this: At the diner where Suzy works, she can serve sorrel soup only on days that begin with the letters *F* or *T*. She can never serve sorrel soup on a day after she's served lentil soup and never before a day when she will serve split pea soup. If she served lentil on Sunday and pea on Wednesday, when can Suzy serve sorrel soup this week?

I just kept thinking: Suzy is really in trouble here!

And: What is sorrel soup?

For 3.5 hours.

UC Davis's creative writing program required a subject test in English literature, for which I was mildly prepared. I minored in English and knew a ton about, oh, three writers, all of whom were twentieth-century women never mentioned on the test. My knowledge of Shakespeare, Chaucer, and Donne was spotty. I survived this three-hour ordeal and was actually pleased that I ended up scoring around the 50th percentile, which says loads about me and my high standards for myself.

Most of the weight of the application rested on the twenty-page fiction sample, which should have been my first clue to my supreme lack of readiness for an MFA program. I possessed not one finished story. Instead I had scraps: dozens of half-written, autobiographical stories that ground to a halt on page six. It was a very odd station in life to have arrived at, this place of certainty that writing was my fate and yet having not one piece of hard evidence to prove it.

I set to work. I typed away, and I balled up pages and threw them on the floor as I'd seen writers do in movies. I wrote about a waitress living in Santa Fe who spent her nonworking hours hanging out with well-educated waitresses talking listlessly about hazy futures and drinking coffee and vodka cranberries. Like *Less Than Zero*, it was written in the terse prose style that is third-generation Hemingway and described the lives of self-important and underemployed youth. Unlike *Less Than Zero*, the characters lived in the middle of the desert without good cars, clothes, or sunglasses. And unlike *Less Than Zero*, the narrator never got into any real trouble because that would require revealing too much about myself. Can we say "best seller"?

A few months later I found out I did *not* get into Davis (you saw that coming, I know). Feeling as if my writer dream had been permanently defeated, I decided to pursue an MA in English literature instead. By that point I had actually gotten up the nerve to move to San Francisco, so I chose San Francisco State by default based on its proximity and willingness to allow anyone with the ability to pay tuition into their MA program.

After just a course or two, I quickly became mired in the nefarious world of literary criticism in which Derrida and Foucault are lords. The year is 1987. Literary criticism has replaced Bordeaux as the most popular French import. No one really knows what they're doing with this loopy French stuff, so it's the Emperor's New Clothes all over the place. We read all the classics but never to admire them. We call the writing "text" and we never say "the writer," we say "the author," but we never talk about the author or what the author intended or might have intended because the author doesn't matter. The author is the mere conduit of text. Text is bigger than the writer because language is born out of power structures that are bigger than the writer. It's political, Baby.

So, for the next two years, I read other writers instead of doing my own writing. I did textual analysis and wrote essays about the text, thereby creating more text. Instead of being a writer, I dated one. And yes, writing the seminar papers caused me a great deal of angst, but I got through them somehow and everything was going well enough until: the Thesis.

To graduate from the master's program, one needed to write a hundred-page thesis. This was something I'd certainly known from the start of the program but had stalled thinking about, the same way one delays thinking about IRA contributions until one's knees give out and about emergency preparedness until the ground is shaking below your feet. But now there was nothing else to do—no more courses to take, no more forms to fill out—except write the thesis, which was always referred to as the Hundred-Page Thesis. Like the Hundred Years' War, its length was never separate from its identity.

After all the collegiality and stressful-but-doable assignments of the courses, I now felt like I'd been marooned on an island and my only means of escape was this daunting task. My sense of isolation doubled overnight when my writer boyfriend broke up with me without warning. Actually, there had been warning, but I'd refused to acknowledge it.

The warning looked like this:

Setting: a Chinese restaurant in San Francisco's Inner Sunset neighborhood on a cold February evening.

WRITER BOYFRIEND (after reading his fortune, which was something like "Everyone loves you and it will always be this way."): So, what's your fortune say?

ME: Oh, um, it's not that interesting.

WRITER BOYFRIEND: Hey, I told you mine. C'mon, what's it say?

ME: Let's see. Okay. It says, "Your lover will never leave you."

WRITER BOYFRIEND: Oh.

So, yes, there was warning, but like with most warnings, there's not much you can do when they arrive but let life play itself out. It might have been nice, though, if the breakup hadn't landed when I was on page eight of the Hundred-Page Thesis.

But now I'd been stuck on page eight for a month. Adding to my mounting stress was the knowledge that every semester that I worked on the thesis would cost more tuition and would delay my plan for moving ahead: leave the waitressing life and get a job teaching at a community college. But even knowing all that couldn't make me write. For three weeks I stared at the eight-page thing. I took it over to the Tart to Tart café on Irving and gnawed on it over lattes and giant muffins. I took it home and tossed it onto the rug and wrestled with it down there for a while before I dragged it back to my desk and tried to get out something—anything—and then finally slumped over my desk in defeat.

I asked the other grad students, but they were either similarly stuck and therefore of no help whatsoever, or just racing along, typing out pages as if they were being dictated from on high.

"Just do it," my friend Margit said. She was twenty-five and already owned a condo somewhere near the end of the BART line, which in itself seemed beyond comprehension. "Tell yourself it's easy."

Easy. Okay. Easy. I told myself that, but myself just answered back that it was easy for Margit. She'd picked a more comprehensible topic. Mine, I knew, was convoluted—a dash of Foucault, a dash of Derrida, a little structuralism, a pinch of post-structuralism, none of which I fully understood. But I'd convinced myself that the topic had to be really hard to prove that I was smart. Though apparently not smart enough to actually write the thesis.

Desperate for help, I called my thesis adviser and told her I wanted to meet.

"You have some pages?" The way she said "pages" seemed ominous. She gave the word a weight one would not employ to reference eight pages.

"Some," I squeaked out, and left the dog-eared eight pages in her mailbox, hoping for a miracle. We met the next week at the Ecumenical House across from the university at the southern edge of the city, where the glamour of San Francisco becomes a stretch of identical, nameless suburbs.

"Is this a draft?" she asked. "A *rough draft*?"

I had no idea how to answer that. I was writing a hundred-page thesis. If we're looking at eight pages, of course those are going to be a "draft." But the way she said "draft," like a cough, something to be cleared from the throat, I understood a draft must be a very bad thing.

She lowered her voice to a rasp. "Don't *ever* give me a rough draft again. Do you understand?"

"I've been having some problems." I thought of the boyfriend business but veered away from that, knowing that her disgust would only be magnified by that getting-your-head-messed-up-over-a-boy sort of nonsense. Yes, we'd broken up just the week before, but I knew this would not fly with this venerable feminist and professor as a reason for not getting your work done. I wondered how bad it would be to cry in front of her, this tall expert on Middle English and Shakespeare. This woman who enjoyed Dryden. Enjoyed! "I've been having some problems," I started again, "managing the project. My time, maybe?"

"I can't help you with that," she said, threading an arm through a coat sleeve. "My job is to help you with the *content*. Get some pages done. *Finished pages*."

On the ride home on the M and N trains, her words rung in my head like some unsolvable puzzle. If her job was to help me with content and I could never come up with content, did that mean I would forever be outside of the scope of help? If she couldn't help me, could *anyone*? Once home, I dropped onto the sofa and sobbed. The jig was up. I wasn't going to be able to do this stupid thesis, which meant the last few years—all the money, energy, and time that went into getting this degree— were wasted. It also meant that I wasn't smart, that I was flawed, essentially and inalterably different from people who completed things, who won prizes and scholarships and had relationships that lasted—people who had One Real Job.

A few days later, I shuffled into the used bookstore on Ninth Avenue around the corner from my apartment. There, a book caught my eye: *Working It Out: 23 Women Writers, Artists, Scientists, and Scholars Talk About Their Lives and Work*. The cover was clearly an artifact of 1970s feminism with its collage of black-and-white photos of women of all races—black women with Afros, fresh-scrubbed women with no makeup and hair that didn't require a professional cut. One sported a bun and a pair of dangling earrings; another sat thoughtfully behind a typewriter.

I flipped through the book quickly and then looked again at the women on the cover, who seemed to form a sort of pragmatic sorority. They reminded me of the women who'd been my undergrad professors, women who'd studied, written, and muscled their way into old-boy academia. Women who had spine-worn copies of *The Second Sex* on their crowded bookshelves. They were the women I'd gone to with every unmet need—for Mommy, for approval, for validation—when I'd arrived at college. They'd let me into their shabby offices and listened to me while I gobbled up their office hours. They took me far more seriously than I took myself. They were the women who showed me a glimmer of who I could be in the world, who showed me that a woman could have a life that revolved around books and ideas.

I looked inside: four dollars. On instinct, I bought it and scurried back to my little apartment.

As I lay on my sofa leafing through *Working It Out*, the tuition meter whirring away in the background, a calm washed over me. I studied the cover's black-and-white pictures of seventies feminists again. I imagined their lives—with lovers and children and pasta dinners made with fresh tomatoes and basil.

I flipped to an essay entitled "Learning to Work" and started with recognition as I read the first paragraph: "A work problem," it stated, "consists of being unable to work, not because of external pressures such as lack of time, but because of internal problems, which can be exacerbated or disguised by external pressures." The essay's writer saw herself not as a blocked writer but as a person with a "work problem," which she defines as "a problem in doing labor that would fulfill the true self." I was pretty sure waitressing was not labor that fulfilled my true self. As little as I'd written and despite all evidence to the contrary, it would seem that my "work," as the writer called it, was writing.

My eyes darted to the photo of the writer, Virginia Valian, on the adjacent page. It showed Valian absorbed in her work, not bothering to look up at the camera, not caring that a city pulsated behind her through a plate-glass window. My gaze shifted to the title again: "Learning to Work." *Learning*. Not knowing already how to work, but *learning*. Hope flickered through me. Maybe, just maybe, I thought, there was a way through this after all.

In the opening pages of the essay, Valian sets the scene: It's Cambridge, 1970; she's done all the coursework and now she just needs to write this pesky dissertation, but she's doing everything but write. (I was *not* the only one after all!) After analyzing her situation, Valian decides that she needs to break her work time into measurable and doable units. She runs through the possibilities of how long she might be able to sit at her desk at a stretch. After an opening bid of three hours, which she quickly rules out, she considers shorter and shorter amounts of work time until finally she settles on fifteen minutes. She could, she decides, work for fifteen minutes at a stretch.

Again I glanced at the photo. This respectable, employed professor was admitting to the world that she saw fifteen minutes of work as a stretch she could *live through*. So not *everyone* was working away so calmly. There were people—well, at least one person—like me out there. A person who'd struck a bargain with herself to work for fifteen minutes. Then I wondered: Could *I* work for fifteen minutes?

I thought maybe I could.

So, *fifteen* minutes. What magic had I stumbled upon? I felt like I'd just been given the permission I'd been waiting for all my life—the go-ahead to work on something for a very tiny amount of time and then to walk away. Ideally, of course, I would eventually not need to walk away after fifteen minutes. Perhaps one day soon the allotted fifteen minutes would be the gateway into a reverie of work from which I would lift my head only to realize that hours had elapsed and a snowbank of pristine, finished pages had risen around me.

With controlled excitement, I read the section of the essay subtitled "Rules and Rationales of the Program" (It was a *program*! It had *rules*! It would *work*!). "The first rule was that the fifteen-minute period had to be spent solely in working." Good, agreed. I could do that. But then, she added a few lines later: "I also had to learn that losing myself in my work was not dangerous." I shivered with recognition but couldn't stop now to think about this work-as-dangerous belief. I had to get my program!

Eager to start my first fifteen minutes, I readied the kitchen timer. But I knew that if I went into the fifteen minutes without a plan, I could choke. Too afraid to use my first fifteen minutes on the actual *writing* of my thesis, I bargained with myself that the first fifteen minutes could be spent on brainstorming a plan for completing the thesis. That seemed fair enough. The timer started and I quickly settled in and used the time making a list of fifteen-minute tasks: Look up this and that; write a paragraph explaining X; read this source. When the timer went off, I felt a surge of disproportionate pride, but I also knew that if I didn't do a writing task *that day*, I'd still be doomed: I'd end up using my new program as a very elaborate form of procrastination. So, after the requisite snacks, tea, and some heavy sighing, I set the timer again and valiantly chose a writing task from the list.

Reader, I wrote. I wrote for fifteen minutes.

It might as well have been a lunar landing, I felt so much joy. The thaw had come after the freeze. Page eight behind me, I typed my way through page nine. The worst was over. Yes, I had no boyfriend and ninety-one pages to write, but I knew after that fifteen minutes that I would continue the fifteen-minute sessions and soon the fifteen minutes would turn into longer periods. By the end of the week, I was working for several hours at a stretch. Probably four hours. Four hours punctuated with lunch and cookies and coffee and trips to the mailbox, but the pages piled up nonetheless.

Two months from that first fifteen-minute session, I entered a small classroom and defended my thesis. I passed. It's possible everyone passes, but so what? It was still my moment of glory. Right after that, I got word that I'd been hired to teach at a community college in southern Utah. But the master's degree and the job played second and third to the most fabulous moment of all when my desk jet printer had spat out the last page of that thesis. Page 96—yes, I'd come in slightly underweight, but still, it was done.

Just then the Clash song "Rock the Casbah" came on the radio. I turned it up and up and up.

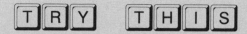

1. Start noticing the times when you stop working. Is it when you get stuck on something? When the writing starts to feel "too hard"? Is it when you get thrown off your routine because something unexpected comes up? Is it when you're on the verge of taking your story to a deeper level? Keep track of your sticking points. You might even want to take a few notes about these stopping patterns.

2. Use the information you've collected against yourself. If you're a writer who stops when the writing gets tough, keep a timer by your desk and set it for five minutes when you feel like stopping. Tell yourself you only need to write for the five extra minutes (but of course, here's hoping you keep going past that). If the unexpected throws you off, keep a notebook in your purse or backpack, and tell yourself you need to find five minutes in your day to write—whether it's waiting at the DMV or at your kid's soccer practice. (I've written in the Costco parking lot with a baby asleep beside me. I've also *not* written when I've had all the time and quiet needed.) You might be surprised what you can write in five minutes: a few sentences, maybe a paragraph, and it might be just the paragraph you've been waiting for.

3. Read Virginia Valian's "Learning to Work" essay online. It's on the Writing Is My Drink blog. Look under the tab "Learning to Work." After reading the essay, write for fifteen minutes on your reaction to the essay. What parts of Valian's experience

could you relate to? What in her method for overcoming her work problem could be helpful to you?

4. Commit to writing fifteen minutes a day for the next two weeks. Keep a log. The log can be anything from a check mark to a few notes about how the writing went. When I did this, I kept a log only because I told my students I would be doing so. Most days I wrote something terse, like "Did it"; but some days I did take notes, and I was stunned to see how many reasons I had for not writing. I love writing. I love having written. I have written a book. I've had work published. I make a living as a writer and a writing teacher. So it would make sense that I would not resist writing for fifteen paltry minutes, but there it was, chronicled in grisly detail: "Too tired." "Don't want to!" "Tired." "Too much to do." Do I spend fifteen minutes every day checking e-mail? Yes. Do I ever say I'm too tired or don't have time? No. But checking e-mail is a passive activity. I do nothing but click and see what others have sent me, how others want me to use my time, my energy, my life. Writing is active. Writing is me forging my own meaning.

5. Disable your Internet capabilities on your writing computer. Or write on an old laptop with no wireless. Or do what I do most of the time: handwrite. There's nowhere to click on my yellow legal pad to get to Facebook. Believe me, I've tried. Write for ten minutes on this question: What do you consider your true work?

6. Twenty years after first reading the "Learning to Work" essay in San Francisco, I found myself in need of its advice again. Once again I was feeling stuck and couldn't get myself back to

the page. Luckily, despite multiple moves and numerous yard sales, I still owned the copy of *Working It Out* that I'd bought in 1989. I dug it out and reread Valian's essay and once again felt inspired to start working again in fifteen-minute increments until I could get my writing momentum back.

7. I realized then how much my writing students could also benefit from this approach and started teaching seminars based on Valian's ideas as well as my own on how to give ourselves—as I learned from Valian—the pleasure of working consistently and incrementally on a project. (That's one of my favorite lines in the essay: "I decided that I wanted to work every day, because I wanted to experience that constancy of working that I had always denied myself.")

8. Have you ever read an essay or a book that immediately helped you? If so, write about the advice you gained from that author and how you applied it.

Part Two

Initiation

4

A Funny Thing
Happened on the Road
to Schema Theory

Although I'd broken through the thesis block, my dream for my "real writing"—whatever *that* might be—was still on hold. Nonetheless, for the first time since I hit puberty, I was neither a student nor a waitress. My freshly printed business cards declared that I was an assistant professor of English. The relief of having a Real Job with tasks that endured beyond the dinner shift—not to mention medical, dental, and vision benefits—more than made up for any ill-defined dream deferred, at least for a good long while.

Nothing, though, prepared me for the terror of my first quarter of teaching. Ostensibly, a master's in English literature is the preparation for teaching English at a community college. But reading Shakespeare's tragedies in your apartment and then writing papers about them or sitting through a lecture on feminist criticism and the Victorian novel is absolutely no preparation whatsoever for standing in front of a class and trying to explain how to support a thesis sentence. No correlation exists between these two activities. It's like thinking that studying botany will prepare you to run a landscaping business. Yes, it's good to know what those plants are doing out there, but let's face it: 95 percent of the time, you're going to be mowing lawns and hefting the lawn mower in and out of the truck.

There is a time-honored disconnect between learning and teaching in higher education. Few graduate students ever take classes in pedagogical theory. The assumption is that if you know your stuff, you'll somehow be able to transmit that stuff to your students. The *how* is your own problem. But in this case, the disconnect between the preparation and the daily work seemed particularly absurd. One of the listed requirements of my new job was a master's degree in English, but the bulk of my job assignment was to teach basic developmental writing as well as a course called Success Skills, a component of the job I remained in denial about until the final days of summer.

Success Skills was part study skills, part resource guide to college life, part learning theory, and part motivational lectures. As the school year rapidly approached, I sweated through the last scorching days of the southern Utah summer, knowing that I was in no way prepared to teach anyone how to succeed in college. I flipped through the highly left-brained accompanying text for the class, aptly named *How to Study in College*, and a hot darkness overtook me. The Cornell Method of notetaking! How to take multiple-choice tests! How to manage your time in college!

My problems with the course content were endless. First, I'd never done half of the things the book recommended one do to succeed and yet had somehow succeeded, although I could not say how. I also did not deep down believe that the answer to success lay in the rigid methods outlined, and if those methods were, in fact, the road to success, then learning and college would be such soulless prospects that I would want nothing to do with them and certainly could not in good conscience recommend anyone else to endure such an uninspired use of time and money. I had gotten through college—it would seem, now that I felt forced to locate the source of my "success"—mostly by taking courses that created an enormous voltage of excitement within me and by dragging myself through the requirements that didn't. But that could never be a recommended route, could it? "So, kids, go for The History of Modern Art and the Harlem Renaissance literature classes and feel free to leave your math requirements to your final year. Then load yourself up on caffeine—diet pills, if you have to—the mornings of those classes and somehow just force your brain to focus on what is being said in the class. Somehow, do the assignments, survive the tests. Yes, you'll get a D, but it's not your major, so no biggie, right?"

Yes, my own absolute lack of method and structure as a student was one of my major problems with the prospect of teaching Success Skills, but something more fueled my resistance, something that I now realized—so late, *too* late!—would certainly undermine not only my ability to teach this course but my ability to teach *anything*.

It dawned on me that I had no faith in my own intelligence. I looked in the mirror and, like the anorexic who can't seem to connect the dropping number on the scale and the reality of her own body, could never seem to connect my academic achievements and my intelligence. Every success seemed like a fluke; every paper that received an A just seemed like another lucky break—maybe because I knew how much anxiety each of those papers had cost me, how much rolling on the floor and gnashing of teeth. If I were truly intelligent, I guess I'd always figured, I would have just whipped them out.

But now I was supposed to be a professor. Good grief! Let the impostor syndrome begin.

My one remaining hope for preparing the Success Skills course was to badger the previous instructor before she fled for California. B. was headed to Stanford to pursue a master's in education. A Caucasian woman with a degree in Chinese languages from Yale, B. appeared to suffer from no intellectual anorexia whatsoever. She was the Anti-Theo. She seemed to have taught the classes here in her sleep; the rest of her time had been devoted to doing whatever she liked, which included running a dude ranch with the guy who'd lured her to Utah. Unlike me, who felt lucky to have this job—to have any job that wasn't waitressing—B. had just filled a short gap here. For a woman as bold, entitled, and outspoken as B., this was a pit stop on the mighty speedway that stretches between Yale and Stanford.

B. talked fast, referencing everything from Alexis de Tocqueville to MTV to jokes about blow jobs. I had mixed feelings about her; she was Glinda, the feminist good witch, and I knew when she left, there'd be no one here who'd understand who I was and how I'd come to be following this yellow brick road. At the same time, I wanted her gone, gone, *gone*. We were a bit like astronauts who'd both traveled off course and run into each other in a far-flung galaxy. You couldn't help but marvel that we were here together in Utah, a state with no measurable reverence or even need for the Professional Woman. But she was Neil Armstrong, and I was one of those guys back in the ship you can't remember the name of, if you ever knew it. Being in a staff meeting with B. dropping by was like finding a photo of a babelicious woman among your boyfriend's papers and having him shrug and say, "Just an old girlfriend." I wanted not only to extinguish her, I also wanted to eradicate all memory of her from the minds of my fellow faculty. But still, I feared her coming departure; once she was gone, my isolation would know no bounds.

We had lunch together at a café in Pioneer Square a few days before she left. She spoke with wild excitement about Jean Piaget, schema theory, and Howard Gardner's theory of multiple intelligences as if all this were the stuff I lived and breathed. Apparently, all these things held the secret underpinnings to my nemesis: the Success Skills course.

"Hold on, let me get this down," I said, digging through my purse for paper.

"Don't worry about it," she said, her mouth half full of salad, waving away my search for paper with her free hand. "It's all on the notecards."

"Notecards?" I asked, hope rising in me for the first time in days.

"Notecards," she said with a wink. "It's all in the cards, my friend. No worries."

The day after B. left for Stanford, I tracked down the file with the note cards. For each of the Success Skills lectures there was a stack of about ten note cards paper-clipped together. I started with the one for Class Three: How We Learn. "In Piaget's schema theory," the card read, "he asserted that our brains are like filing cabinets." Okay, I thought, fair enough. The next card read, "For each topic, we own a folder, which may be very thin or quite full."

The cards lacked the promise of revealing the mystery of Success Skills I'd hoped they'd deliver. But I was also tired of being afraid, of thinking about the dreaded class, of preparing for something I didn't truly know how to prepare for. I'd read the corresponding chapters in Pauk and Owens's *How to Study in College*; bring the cards and it would work out, right? B. had done it, hadn't she?

I overlooked the fact that B. had created these notes based on her own knowledge, which was immense. Each of the minuscule notations on each individual card pointed to a large file in her brain that she would download when prompted by each tiny note. I had no such files in my brain. I had only the tiny note pointing to my vast ignorance of how we learn and many other subjects.

Enrollment in the Success Skills class was mandatory for students participating in a certain scholarship-generating grant program. No typical college student would take such a course otherwise. My first quarter of Success Skills was taught in an auditorium of seventy-seven freshmen in which I couldn't make out the faces in the darkness of the top rows. When the fated day arrived, I stumbled into the first class, blinded by the bright stage lights. I began my rambling Welcome to the

Class! speech, never letting my eyes stray above the third row. I'd never taught a class in my life, but to let that on would guarantee a bloodbath. All power would instantly be transferred to the sharks; I'd be destroyed.

The class met twice a week for ten weeks, and I got through each class, but just barely. I clung to the note cards and made up all sorts of stuff, to the point where I thought I might be arrested and run out of town. I made a lot of jokes and, frankly, the class was easy, so most of the students liked me well enough. But I knew the class wasn't *good*. Then it came: course evaluation day.

Let me pause for a moment and say this: Yes, in most jobs, one is evaluated, but there is only one job in which one is evaluated *anonymously* by a group in which the median age is 18.75 years.

The evaluations came back to me a few weeks later, and it was quickly clear that this wasn't the most discerning group. Except for the occasional gripe, they were happy enough. A few people had things to say about my hair and shoes. But there was one evaluation that jumped from the pile. "Let go of the cards," the young evaluator wrote in loopy cursive. "You know this stuff. You just have to *trust* yourself. Just put down the cards and tell us what *you* know. You'll do great. I promise!!!"

Let go of the cards. I felt so naked, so revealed. It began to occur to me that every job has an unspoken emotional requirement that, while never listed among the qualifications in any job description, is just as vital to one's success as those that are. Doctors have to be able to cope with facing the grief of others; lawyers have to be willing to assert themselves even when they don't feel like it. Teachers have to feel the exposure of all eyes on them, of being the starting spot for everything in the room. Writers have to make themselves vulnerable by sharing their opinions. You can be a genius and still not be up for teaching if the emotional requirements of the job—including the ability to handle this exposure—are beyond your reach.

The next quarter I began to loosen my grip on the cards a little. One thing I noticed about the cards was they made me feel like crap. Life with the cards involved me following a very loose script instructing me on how to impersonate B., a person who cared about a different set of things than I cared about, which is easy for me to say now. But mostly, back then, the cards reminded me of all I felt I should know if I were ever going to be half the teacher I imagined B. had been.

Occasionally, I found myself putting the cards aside, and then I'd tell a little story about when I was in college, about how I'd felt afraid and unprepared most of the time. I'd blush as I told these stories, but I noticed that when I did, the students would actually begin to wake up, and sometimes they'd laugh and sometimes they'd even tell stories about themselves, about their experiences in the classroom. The note cards gradually fell into disuse as I brought in research about learning meaningful to me, but a large part of the class became stories: stories of barely getting by, stories of succeeding unexpectedly, stories of finding your passion and the topics you can learn without strain.

Even though I still wanted to prove to my students, my fellow faculty, and myself that I was a real academic, that I was as hard-core as B., the truth—revealing itself in the classroom as gravity reveals itself in every object that falls—was that I am not truly of the academy. My strength does not lie in the rigors of research or in the dogged pursuit of knowledge or information. The truth, which I still wanted to deny, is that I am far too erratic and silly to be a true academic. But it was also dawning on me that this might actually make me *more* suited for the job at hand, and that a true academic might not be interested in working for long in this particular trench of higher education. Case in point: B. was gone.

I also began to realize that I shared a special bond with the majority of my students in rural Utah: We doubted our own smarts. Most of my students' parents hadn't gone to college. This, the department head told me, made them "high risk" for not completing their own college degrees. I nodded. This made sense and made me want to help them. Why didn't it occur to me then that neither my mother nor my biological father had finished high school? I could understand what "high risk" meant in terms of my students, but I had never been able to see myself as falling short for any reason other than my own failings.

As my first year of teaching came to a close, the class no longer looked much like the course B. had taught. It wasn't any better or worse, but now it was mine. I was my own kind of teacher and no longer simply an impersonator of a person I believed could do the job better than I could.

As it turns out, many of the lessons of teaching are also the lessons of writing, with both tasks entirely dependent on your confidence in your own material, point of view, and voice. In the classroom, the teacher's voice is the thread that stitches the pieces together, that takes the jumble of readings, activities, and discussion and renders them into knowledge. The class relies on the teacher's ability to make the parts cohere, just as the reader depends on the writer to make the disparate parts of a story unify. But unlike writing, which allows the writer to do the work of unification on the writer's own timetable, teaching demands that you get your act together *now*, in front of everyone. There isn't much room in the classroom for the teacher's crisis of faith, "intellectual anorexia," or doubt in any other shape or form. In the classroom, all eyes are on *you*.

Teaching two to three classes a day five days a week, I found myself in a boot camp for confidence, a "scared straight" program for doubters. Some days I faltered, others I didn't, but every day it was my job to teach and so I did. It got easier. I still felt nauseated the first day of a new quarter, but my confidence in my voice grew, and having gained that confidence at metaphorical gunpoint in the classroom prepared me to face my doubts in myself as a writer. The lesson of learning to put down the cards and trust myself was essential to finding my voice on the page, and soon I would have an opportunity to use that new knowledge.

Living in Utah was a complicated experience for me. Even though I'd felt like an outsider most of my life, all that garden-variety alienation was child's play compared to living in a culture with secret rituals and underwear, a place where old folks with little suitcases walked into the giant white temple to do who knows what. A place where coffee is *not* on the menu. Part of me was always at odds with Utah's culture, but living in Utah also freed me. No longer surrounded by strivers and creative types haunted by a feeling of falling behind, I now resided among people who were either tremendously talented at hiding their lust for more or who were, in fact, fairly satisfied with their lives.

Life in southern Utah is M-E-L-L-O-W, especially if one is not Mormon and therefore not expected to go to Relief Society meetings or have Family Home Evenings or attend church services for three hours at a stretch. Plus, all this mellowness is happening against a backdrop of red canyons, long mesas, and the bluest sky imaginable. Hours after my arrival in the state, I stood in the middle of the red and white rock of Snow Canyon State Park and thought I'd never heard such quiet. I felt an odd sensation wash over me that I thought might be what the less anxious must call "peace."

After spending the last two and half years primarily indoors reading, I now lived in a place that insisted that I go outside, a place where it seemed like enough to just exist. Once I established a teaching routine, I began to relax in this land of very few demands. I biked up and down the empty streets of my new small town on Sunday mornings. I hiked. I rode in a two-seater plane over canyons inaccessible by car. I caught exactly one fish. I made apricot jam and planted tomatoes. Sometimes, I'd think: I should try to write. And then I'd take a nap.

I felt like the upward push of my twenties had landed me in a big warm desert resting spot. I now watched TV and slept when a year earlier I would've been reading something way over my head, but now I had a *job*, a *career*, which implied that all the reading and studying and sweating over seminar papers on Shelley's *Frankenstein* had led me out of the wilderness of eternal poverty and identity-crushing restaurant work. In San Francisco, I'd always been strapped for cash, sleep, and time, schlepping in the fog from my tutoring job, via two trains and a cable car, to my waitressing gig in North Beach. Now I slept eight hours a night and commuted ten minutes through hushed desert to get to work.

Within a year of my arrival in Utah, I began to acknowledge that my stay there wasn't a temporary one. Yes, my spiritual and political beliefs might've separated me from the pack, but increasingly my life resembled that of the locals. Within another year, I married a transplant from California. Six months later we bought a house and then, of course, next came the inevitable dog. A job, a husband, a house, a dog, and somewhere in there I turned thirty: My footloose, angst-y twenties were officially over.

Inevitably, the novelty of the peaceable kingdom waned, though, and restlessness and ambition soon flickered again. After work, I'd walk our dog along the red dirt roads that traversed the terrain of black volcanic rubble and silvery blue sage across the street from our house. Beyond the lava and the sage, stacks of the white and red rock formed a very surreal park called Snow Canyon. Walking through this landscape, I'd feel my dream of becoming a writer resurfacing, a force gathering critical mass. I still had this idea that one day I would do something I thought of as my "real writing," although the hubris of this aspiration also embarrassed me because I had no proof that I could write and no idea what form this "real writing" would take. Haiku? Fiction? All I knew was that I wasn't doing it.

On the few occasions I did try to write, I wrote short stories that inevitably ground to a halt after five pages or so. Some segue or momentum of plot usually tripped me up. After that, I'd squeak out a sentence or two but my heart wasn't in it, and so I'd give up. I had a few notebooks full of false starts. The busy school years blurred past in a rush of students' questions, papers, and class prep, but during the long, hot summers off work the feeling of falling behind would start up again. The years were going by, I told myself: Ticktock, as if writing had a closing biological window.

One day a woman in the HR department at the college told me about an annual summer writers' retreat in the mountains above Cedar City, and I decided to go. Up a twisty road of pines and red rock, an old lodge held a number of classes all about the craft of writing, really nutsy and boltsy how-to classes. One class I took that week, taught by the poet Ken Brewer, changed everything for me as a writer.

Ken was a sweet bear of a man who was a product of the very best parts of the seventies—the groovy aspects that supported equality, vegetable gardens, and self-expression. As he segued into our writing assignment, Ken talked about how he always had trouble sticking to external forms. He gave the example of learning to waltz, which he'd found very difficult. He could dance free form to rock and roll, he told us, because then he didn't have to stick to someone else's pattern of how his body should be moving. As I nodded yes, yes, yes, he parlayed this analogy into talking about how he'd finally discovered a form that was perfectly suited to his content. He told us that this form he called "the triptych" had helped him to find himself as a writer.

Ken taught us that the triptych's structure, a form borrowed from visual art, grows out of theme instead of story. Instead of beginning with a story you want to tell, you start with an idea or a feeling, he explained as he led us in a writing exercise that required us to isolate a concept, feeling, idea, or theme we wanted to write about.

Everything he was saying about the triptych made sense to me. I felt this tremendous sense of relief and joy, as if I'd been traveling for years in a country where no one spoke my language, and I'd finally met someone who understood me perfectly. As I worked on the theme-identifying exercise, it occurred to me that often my need to write sprung from the desire to express an idea or a feeling rather than the need to tell a specific story. I quickly identified that I wanted to write about a long-standing sense of separation I felt and my craving to heal that sense of separation. Ken urged us to pick a single word and I chose this word: "detachment."

As instructed by Ken, I wrote the word "detachment" in the center of a page. Then, following his direction that we come up with three events or moments that matched this feeling or theme, I named in separate bubbles two scenes from my childhood, and the final scene was the day I moved away from home at seventeen. Ken explained that these three scenes would become the triptych's three panels, and when hung together they would tell a story larger than the sum of its panels. Magic, Ken called it.

Ken urged us to write those three scenes right then and there. And so we did. We sat there in silence in the cavernous mountain lodge at four thousand feet with the smell of pine in the room, writing. I wrote one scene and then another and then another. As I wrote, I fell into the story in a way I never had before, because I trusted Ken and I trusted this form. In this perfect storm of trust and pine and high elevation, I moved into the belief that the story I was writing *would* come together and that, gulp, I would finish it.

At the end of the day, I drove down that twisty mountain road back to my house in the red desert and fired up my laptop. I typed up what I'd written in class. A single golden thread of the theme of detachment wove its way through the three scenes— just as Ken had said it would—magically holding the scenes together, but just barely. It was the barely that thrilled me. *Barely* was exactly what I was trying to say; maybe *barely* was what I'd been wanting to say for a while. Maybe I'd been waiting to find the right form. Maybe we're all waiting for the right form.

In part, the triptych worked for me because it lent a structure that was a natural extension of what I felt compelled to say. I'd been yearning to express how seemingly disparate moments in my life were united by a theme and a feeling—for a way of *showing* how those moments were united instead of just simply saying that they were. The magic of the triptych sprung from the empty spaces between the scenes, negative spaces that seemed to whisper their own quiet message.

It was a small accomplishment, but it's often our small accomplishments that give us the confidence to keep going—to do more, to write more, to explore further. Finally I'd completed a personal narrative, the writing I dared to call my own, to call— even though I felt foolish to do so—my "real" writing.

I went on to write more triptychs. Okay, the truth is I became hooked on triptychs. Some twenty years later, I'm still teaching my memoir-writing students the triptych form, and the form continues to thrill me with its ability to tell a new type of story. Like me, many of my students feel the triptychs are the first pieces they've written that felt complete.

The inspiration to finish that first triptych in that Utah lodge was more than arriving upon the perfect form; the other piece of magic I got from that workshop was the understanding that my life was worth observing, worth the ink and the paper, worth examination and time, and was, in essence, of literary value. Even though the word "memoir" wasn't used that day, the examples Ken gave were autobiographical. As a poet, he was adept at transforming his ordinary experiences into a literary form, and so for him it was natural to use his own experiences in the triptych as well. When I'd written fiction in college, I not only tried to press my square-peg stories into a Hemingway-shaped story form, I often tried to obscure their autobiographical roots, assuming that my life was not the sort of life that could yield up literature. I'd never fought a bull or stepped foot in Manhattan or fly-fished or fought in a war.

One of the essential characteristics of a writer is the willingness and ability to see the stories in our lives and to believe that our observations, thoughts, and obsessions are worth following to the page. If you're accustomed to discounting your thoughts, this valuing your own experience isn't going to happen overnight. It will be a process, a long retraining in which we move from negating to valuing. It has been for me.

I see this process at work each year when a new group of students arrives in my classroom. Often, at the beginning of the year, at least some of them are struggling to believe that their subject matter has value. At the start of fall quarter last year, a student shyly told me that she felt self-conscious that her topic was not important enough or maybe somehow self-indulgent.

"What is it, the topic?" I asked in a whisper, anticipating something like the joy of teacup collecting.

"Deciding whether to have kids or not," she said weakly.

"You're not sure if the decision to bring life into the world is big enough?"

She nodded.

I urged her, maybe even begged her, to write on that topic. "Begged" sounds extreme, but I am rabid about this issue, because I can very easily remember that time when I didn't think my own life-and-death topics were worthy, even when I could read another writer's five-page account of playing Frisbee and think it was funny and fantastic, when it never would have occurred to me to question the value of his topic.

Consider that you are developing bit by bit the habit of believing that your own thoughts are worth exploring. You are cultivating the faith that these thoughts will yield up something, even if you don't know what yet. You're trusting that there will be something of value in there. Even if you feel silly, like you're wasting time on those thoughts now, someday you won't feel silly. That day will come after you've followed the trail of your observations and watched them become something and after you've worked on that something until it becomes golden: a poem that captures the moment, maybe even a painting that matches a feeling or an essay that gives voice to a story only you can tell.

1. Make a list of all the jobs you've ever had.

2. Pick as many of these jobs as you like and for each one list "the emotional requisites" of the job, the emotional task or tasks that the job required you to accomplish. For example, teaching requires exposure and therefore vulnerability.

3. Pick one of these jobs and at least one emotional requisite for that job. Set the timer for ten minutes and write about that job and what it required of you. Did you resist the requirement at first? What did that look like? How did you grow and improve?

4. Write on this question: What did you learn in that job emotionally that could help you as a writer?

5. If you want, continue with this pattern, writing about each of the jobs on your list.

6. Write about a job for which the emotional requisite was overwhelming to you. Perhaps you left the job or stayed but remained miserable because of the burden of the emotional requisite.

7. Write about a time when you took a big risk—such as moving to a new place—so that you could follow a dream.

8. Write for ten minutes on this question: When have you "put down the cards" and started following your own script instead of someone else's?

9. Now consider this: As a writer what would it look like for you to "put down the cards"?

10. Get a small notebook that you keep in your purse or back pocket. Start taking notes on your thoughts and observations. Challenge yourself to take at least one note every day.

11. Go to WritingIsMyDrink.com and read examples of triptychs.

12. Create a triptych of your own, following these instructions or making your own way there.

- Brainstorm a list of ideas/feelings/concepts that you might write on. A partial list of the topics my students have used includes: redemption, loss, grief, love, lust, hope, faith, envy, jealousy, rejection, land, birth, dating. But go for it and generate a list of your own.

- Pick a topic from the list. When choosing, I advise you to go where the heat is, to one of these topics that exhilarates you or even scares you. Personal writing is best when the stakes are high for the writer.

- Follow the clustering technique outlined in the last chapter, brainstorming as much as you can on your topic.

- Write three "panels," ensuring that each panel is somehow tied to the chosen theme. The panels don't have to be the same length.

- Try different orders for the panels before settling on a final version.

- Create segues, an introduction, and a conclusion.

- Spend some time revising your triptych until you are satisfied with it.

5

Writing Together

The image of the lonely writer has never sat well with me. I'm a person who can talk a big free-spirit game but who dreads isolation. My ideal work situation is doing my own thing with a crowd swirling nearby—just in case. The possibility of attention is right there on tap, whether I end up using it or not. No one really uses the word "garret" anymore the way they did when I was growing up. It always sent a small shot of terror through me. If you said you wanted to be a writer back then, someone would inevitably say something like "Oh, you'll be the lonely writer typing away in your garret," which immediately made me want to do anything but write. I have sometimes fantasized about writing in isolation, but as soon as I was in the island cabin or the rented office space (twice I've gone to the trouble of renting and furnishing an office—ugh), I began thinking that maybe it was time to go get a cappuccino somewhere. At one time I thought this resistance was a sign of weakness, an indication that I would never be a real writer. But I'm over that.

In fact, some of the most contented times of my life have involved writing with another person or with a group of people. These have been times when the two driving forces in my life—the need for companionship and the need for self-expression—have converged, the lamb and the lion down for an afternoon nap.

Even if I'm not the one writing, I feel a certain peace whenever two or more people are gathered to write together. In my memoir class, there is usually an in-class writing time. After the initial shuffling of papers, a hush falls over the room as the students bow over their notebooks. Watching them—this collection of people who by day work as attorneys, doctors, receptionists, teachers, mothers—I feel a maternal, protective peace as they write, wanting to keep away anyone who might disturb their time. This time belongs to them. This is their time to write together. Afterwards, yes, you can have them back to answer phones, fill out forms, and wipe noses, but first let them have this.

One hot day during my third summer in Utah, I saw a flyer in the grocery store advertising a writing class in someone's home. The teacher was a poet named Rose. I took a tab with the phone number, and a week later I was sitting cross-legged on the floor of a trailer that smelled of Indian cotton and scented candles in the middle of the desert. We wrote words and phrases on scraps of paper and put them in a bowl. We took turns choosing words from the bowl and then we all sat in silence, scribbling madly on our pads of paper, prompted by the words from the bowl and the presence of each other. If I'd been at home trying to write—which I hardly ever was—I'd probably just be staring at the blank page, but here the urgency to write was palpable and I wrote with a fury.

As we settled into our writing, a warm breeze blew in and the sounds of the desert evening came through the open windows. An engine turning over, a birdcall, a screen door falling shut, followed by feet coming down some steps—wooden steps. Life was buzzing in and out of the room like breath. A room full of strangers, we sat silent, barely yet intensely aware of each other—and there was nothing awkward about it. In fact, it was magical. When I think of that time now—and the many like it I've had since—the word that comes to mind is "communion." We were each fully engaged in our own work and yet undeniably connected to each other.

The feeling I had writing in that poet's trailer was one of genuine contentment. I was doing the work I wanted to do, but in the company of others. I was following a thought but not up the dark, lonely alley I'd always believed was my gauntlet to run if I were ever to become a true writer.

Writing in the poet's trailer in the middle of a red desert surrounded by a small circle of writers, the sound of their pens scratching against paper, I caught a glimpse of another way, a way to be engaged with my work and with others at the same time. This moment seared a possibility into me, and after that I sought to re-create this experience of creative intimacy.

This need for this communion became more acute after my first daughter, Natalie, was born in 1994. Before Natalie, I'd bus-

ied myself with work during the school years and travel during the summers, but now I was home more, still working but
less focused on work. Around this time, my friend Sara from
my Santa Fe waitressing days invited me to become part of a
through-the-mail writing group. Once a month one of us would
mail out a writing prompt along with the writing assignments
the nine of us had written the previous month. Most of the writers were friends of friends I'd never met before, with alluring
addresses like Martha's Vineyard and Topanga Canyon. Each of
us in the group longed to write but were without an audience,
and so we became each other's audience.

One month I opened the manila envelope and found the
writing assignment "A Holy Place." Natalie was playing beside
me on the carpet with blocks and an empty laundry soap con-
tainer. Beyond her, beyond the large living room window, the
red and white rock stacks of Snow Canyon rose up in the horizon. My life, with my new family in this amazing landscape,
suddenly felt very much like a holy place, and so I wrote about
that. It was the first poem I'd completed since I was a freshman
in college. A month later I crossed the street to the mailbox and
pulled out another manila envelope, this one stuffed with stories
and poems of the holy places that belonged to my new group of
writers.

My next experience of writing with others was thornier and
yet more compelling because it involved a group of people who
didn't like each other very much: my community college's humanities department. With six years in Utah behind me, I had
now started mourning the loss of the urbane like a lost limb.
Homesick not so much for a particular place as a particular type

of person. I longed for chance encounters with the like-minded. I ached for someone to reference Jean-Paul Sartre in a joking way. The novelty of my stranger-in-a-strange-land status had passed. I wanted more. I wanted out. I'd applied for a sabbatical for the coming year and was waiting to hear if that would come through. I struggled, though, with what I'd do with the year off if I were to actually get it. I knew that the college's expectation would be that I'd work toward a PhD or MEd, but I dreamed that the year off would be my chance to write creatively. I kept that dream mostly to myself because I didn't want anyone to take it away from me.

Although no one in the humanities department seemed to feel much connection to anyone else, my alienation seemed more acute, since I was one of the few women in the department in a state where people ask "How many children do you have?" instead of "Do you have children?" I was also the instructor in charge of the pre-college-level writing course, which meant that within our self-important department I had the status of a deep-fry cook.

Sometime in late November a memo was sent out: This year we were to spend a week of our hallowed Christmas break together at a faculty development workshop. Oh, joy to the world! Spending a week trapped in a conference room with some of these people was akin to heading off to a desert island with Rush Limbaugh. My mind searched for escape hatches as my eyes scanned down the page, snagging on the name of the facilitator: Terry Tempest Williams. Could this be true?

This was 1996. Terry was still relatively unknown, and it wasn't beyond the scope of possibility that she would be coming to Podunk, Utah, for a week. She is, after all, a Utahan. Terry might have been unknown to many still, but the arrival of Terry Tempest Williams in my small-pond world held special meaning to me. One day about six months prior I'd been driving by some alfalfa fields south of town toward the walking trail that runs along the Virgin River out near the Utah-Nevada line. Punching the radio's buttons, I came upon this woman's voice, a voice rich with conviction and intelligence. I looked at the dial: the NPR station out of Salt Lake City. Who was this woman?

She talked about the importance of place, the importance of digging in where you are, knowing your world, your environment. She could have been talking about anything—the week's weather report. It was her voice I heard: the voice of a woman in full possession of herself, a woman who knows she has power in the world and isn't afraid to use it. The voice, I later found out, belonged to Terry. Hearing her voice as I drove through this beautiful landscape of red cliffs and green irrigated fields, a place that had never seemed like mine to "dig into," I began to feel less alone.

And now she was coming *here*.

The first day of the event, the petulant faculty of the humanities department shuffled in with all the vigor of a chain gang heading out for a day's labor. None of our group of twelve wanted to be there. The room—a large conference room with one long table—offered no diversions or means of escape. We all had empty notepads in front of us, and we all stared at them to avoid eye contact with each other. Then Terry came in the room. I liked her instantly. She wore a jean jacket, a big colorful scarf, no makeup. A few shots of gray defiantly streaked through her brown hair. Everything about her appearance suggested that our tawdry office politics would be exposed and destroyed in her presence. She wasn't an academic. She was a *writer*.

Terry wordlessly took her seat and then began. She was glad to be here, she said. This was the area she called home. Our theme for the week would be "The Importance of Place." Everyone nodded.

She then told us it was time for a quiz. The ten questions of the quiz were all about the physiographic region where we lived, the Colorado Plateau. She asked us to name three animals, three plants, and three birds indigenous to the area. She asked us where our water came from and where our garbage ended up. I began to sweat and shift in my seat, dreading the possibility of being the most ignorant person in the room. I knew a plant or two, let's just say that.

I needn't have worried. After we finished, Terry led us through the questions, gently searching the room for answers. A few of the group did fairly well. Humbled, the rest of us—including those who'd tortured the group with their intellectual smugness in many a department meeting—were all in the remedial class together.

The point of the seminar wasn't to learn about the environment of the area, though—it was to explore our own relationship to place—so Terry began asking us questions about our memories of nature, of growing up, of our families, and after each question we wrote. We wrote in silence under the buzz of fluorescent lights. We were a group that had rarely done anything together but argue. We'd avoided each other at picnics and the annual graduations, and now we sat in a soft silence, the only sounds in the room the occasional cough and the comforting scratch of pens on paper.

After we wrote, Terry asked us to volunteer to read our pieces. The first time no one volunteered, so finally she called on someone. And then another reader stepped up and then another. The pieces were full of the red rock and silvery blue sage and the long tabletop mesas that surrounded the college. They were stories of fishing with grandfathers and visiting poor relatives in failing mining towns. A few of the men cried when they read their pieces. One man gestured that he couldn't read any further into his piece, and Terry softly reassured him that he could. And he did. By Tuesday afternoon, the room had softened. By Wednesday afternoon, we were a group. That night Terry stood in front of an auditorium of people and read from her book *Refuge* about the women in her family who've died of cancer, the price the people of southern Utah have paid for living downwind of the nuclear test site in Nevada. Her words filled the room; the temperature rose. As she read, I thought nothing in the world seemed as important as speaking your mind on the page.

We were exhausted by the next afternoon when Terry gave us our final prompt: Where is home? We wrote and wrote, filling pages and pages of our notebooks. I wrote about not truly having one home, about displacement, about moving and restlessness, about my father shuttling between California, Mexico, and Vietnam throughout my childhood, and about how my mother had emigrated from Canada to California and back in search of love and money. I was buoyed up by the group, unafraid to explore the dark territories that usually frightened me off. If they kept writing, I would too. I felt like I could write forever.

Finally, Terry called time, but this time instead of asking us to read right away, she urged us to work on our assignments at home. That night I wrote with a feeling of purpose I'd rarely experienced before; my writing mattered because someone was waiting for it, a person for whom I wanted to write, an audience that was more than theoretical. I wasn't writing into an abyss. I was writing for Terry. The next morning we read our pieces one by one while Terry listened with the attention of a cat watching birds. She scribbled as we read. Finally, when the last reader had finished, Terry cleared her throat and read a poem that incorporated the best phrases from each of our pieces. It was a tremendous poem. In her clear voice, we were one and we could hear it.

And then all the writing together was over. For our last afternoon together, Terry took us birding down by the Virgin River. We tramped through the bare trees around the edge of the river, the river that united us. We were more alike than I'd wanted to believe. I knew that now, but I also knew that I'd soon be leaving. Wherever I ended up, I would be there to write.

TRY THIS

1. Invite a writing friend to write with you for an hour or two. This is a very companionable way to get some work done. I meet with another writer regularly for a few hours of writing together. We usually meet in a café and spend the first half hour or so chatting about our writing lives and our careers (not usually about the writing itself) and the rest of the time we write in silence. It's very harmonious, and when I'm with her, I often do some of my best work.

2. Explore writing classes you can take in your area. A literary center? An extension program at a university? A continuing education class at a community college? Or maybe there are writers in your area who hold workshops and writers' retreats in their homes.

3. Consider taking a trip to visit a writers' retreat or conference. Or apply for a residency. The Poets & Writers website is a great resource for contact information and submission guidelines: http://www.pw.org/.

4. Write with your kids or someone else's. I wish I did this more often. It's happened a few times spontaneously when I was working on my laptop in the living room, and my two daughters flopped on sofas and began working on their own writing. Young kids are great because they haven't caught on that writing is hard. They just think writing is "fun." One time I requested it on my birthday: an hour of family, writing together. It was one of the best presents. Ever.

5. Start a writing group. Writing groups can be structured in a number of ways ranging from groups that take turns distributing their work for critiques before the meeting to groups that simply write together. If you're planning on a group that will give feedback, it's a good idea to put some forethought into how the group will be structured. There are a number of books out there on writing groups, including *Writing Alone, Writing Together: A Guide for Writers and Writing Groups* by Judy Reeves.

6. Set your timer for fifteen minutes and write using Terry Tempest Williams's prompt "Where is home?"

7. One of the images around the word "writer" that I held in my coming-of-age years was of someone who could live and work in total isolation and who did not need the reassurance of others to keep writing. Because I knew that I could never live up to that image, I believed I couldn't ever become a writer. (I also thought I had to be male to be a "real" writer.)

   Think about what preconceptions and images the word "writer" conjures up for you. What were the images you held of "a writer" in your childhood? Are any of those images limiting you still? Write for ten minutes on this topic.

8. Write for ten minutes about where you grew up. If you grew up in more than one place, as I did, write about each of those places for ten minutes apiece.

9. Answer this question for each of the places you grew up: How did that place contribute to your sense of yourself as a creative person? Was your creativity encouraged and stimulated there, or were you shamed for your creative impulses? Or was it some combination of encouragement and shame?

10. Write about a place that you love for ten minutes. Go for the detail. What about that place inspires you?

11. Write about a place that you loved when you were a kid.

12. Make a list of times when you've been part of a group or a team. Pick a time when you had a transformative experience with a group and write about that for ten minutes.

13. Make a list of times you felt isolated and another list of times you felt part of a community. Pick a time from each list and write about them together.

6

Ginger Harper Died for My Sins

You see, in my view a writer is a writer not because she writes well and easily, because she has amazing talent, because everything she does is golden. In my view a writer is a writer because even when there is no hope, even when nothing you do shows any sign of promise, you keep writing anyway.

—Junot Díaz

A month before the seminar with Terry, my grandma JoJo died of a stroke. She was found in her drafting room taking a nap, the magazine beside her open to an article on Islam. Fresh dirt clung to her gardening shoes outside the kitchen door—further evidence that she'd spent the last day of her eighty-six years well. I felt the loss of her acutely, though, for she was someone who'd understood my lifelong yearning for a big life of authentic expression. JoJo showed me that an artist is a person who makes art and a writer a person who writes and that your love of doing the work exists separately from whatever value anyone else might place on the work. Now that I had decided to finally use my sabbatical to pursue my dream and apply for MFA programs, I would need to remember this lesson.

Growing up, I'd counted on JoJo to show up for me in all the ways that my mother couldn't—not because my mom didn't want to but because her love for a married man and her drinking drew her away from the present moment, the place where children dwell. When I looked into my mother's beautiful blue eyes, I saw a vacancy, a desire for something that was far away. My mother was also distracted by running her business, which was both a necessity and a passion, which pointed to one of the ways that my mother and I essentially differ, although it would take me decades to see and understand this as simply a difference. While I see the world in stories and feelings, my mother sees the world in numbers. When my mom and I talk, she wants to know my numbers: the day's temperature, my mortgage interest rate, the reading on my car's odometer, my weight.

JoJo, on the other hand, lived alongside me, seeing the world through a lens of imagination and creativity in her little pink stucco bungalow on Finger Avenue in Redwood City, California. Whenever I arrived at her door, I knew her face would light up. By the time she was fifty-five, she had three marriages behind her (the family average), and although she still kept company with one of her former husbands from time to time, she had, for the most part, turned her focus from relationships to art, landscaping, playing canasta, and, eventually, to writing. She was home most days, working in her garden or her art studio or at her drafting table or loom. Like her sister, the Zen Buddhist Pat, JoJo knew how to navigate solitude. She lived the last thirty years of her life alone and never seemed too concerned about it. "I found sex awfully repetitive," she told me once when I was twenty-three.

JoJo's approach to the world excited my imagination. It was JoJo who taught me about the missions that stretch along California's spine, dotting the El Camino Real every twenty miles from San Diego to Sonoma. "A day's walk apart," she told me. I could picture the monks in robes like Saint Francis walking steadily from mission to mission, just as I could imagine myself beside JoJo in her white Buick Skylark with the top down, driving from mission to mission. The farther south we drove, the further we'd go back in time until my California—the groovy California of the 1960s—magically transformed into the Golden State of her youth. In her stories, California belonged to Steinbeck, John Muir, and Henry Miller, a legendary, fertile kingdom where orchards spilled into orchards and dirt roads puffed a cloud of burnt sienna dust behind us as the Buick became the black Model T her father bought her in 1924 to drive to Calistoga High School.

I'd often stay at JoJo's on the weekends my mom would go out of town. It would take a long time for me to realize where my mom had been on those weekends—even years after my older sister said, "Of course, he was married! What did you think?" Before my mom would leave for I did not know where, she and I would wend our way toward JoJo's, up El Camino with its neon martini glasses flashing and forever spilling onto the word COCKTAILS, El Camino with its liquor stores that smelled of cardboard and Dubble Bubble, its gas stations and endless cheap motels.

When my mom and I hit Redwood City, we'd turn onto Whipple Avenue, past the Wienerschnitzel hot dog restaurant and the Shaws ice cream parlor and then left at the AAA office onto Finger Avenue. Down Finger Avenue at number 173 stood JoJo's bungalow, with the lime and apricot trees in the back and in the front, the modern, water-efficient landscaping that once was featured in *Sunset* magazine. This was where JoJo wove wall hangings made of sticks, feathers, and dog fur (Samoyed, to be precise), ran her landscape design business, and opened her doors to the occasional undocumented worker to live in her guest room. JoJo was the grandmother who thought coloring books were immoral and that you should definitely know about Picasso by the age of seven. She was my dad's mother. I had almost no relationship with my biological father, Ted Nestor, but it never occurred to me that it was special or strange or amazing that JoJo made our relationship continue and flourish despite his complete disinterest in being my parent.

Together, we ate vanilla ice cream in small glass bowls with silver spoons and played War at the picnic table in her dining room. The phone rarely rang. The occasional car rumbled by. There was nowhere we were supposed to be; we were at the center of a universe of two. Nothing competed for our attention.

During the JoJo weekends stuff got *made*: batik sheets, tie-dyed T-shirts, apricot jam, wool spun from dog hair, elaborate stories about assertive princesses, crazy stitching on homemade pillows in the shape of fish, pictures made with crayons melted on wax paper. Many afternoons at JoJo's were spent in the backyard making batiks. JoJo made me believe that it was the most normal thing in the world to be painting designs with hot wax onto old sheets stretched taut across wooden frames. Much of this stuff we made together most would call *art*, but JoJo resisted the word "artist."

"I make art," she corrected. "Everyone can make art. Some people choose not to." She was the same grandmother who told me sternly when I was nine: "You can have things or freedom. If you don't deliberately choose, you'll be stuck with things."

JoJo modeled for my childhood self the sheer joy of creativity, but I'd spent most of my adult life forgetting what I'd learned from her, focusing on the merit others assigned to my work instead of the pleasure it had to offer me. The competing roles of creator and critic forever split me in two. In the book *What It Is*, cartoonist Lynda Barry describes the problem perfectly when she contrasts the "floating feeling" she had as a child, drawing and creating stories, with the doubts that have plagued her as a working artist. Barry says two questions have beleaguered her and interrupted her enjoyment of her creative process: "Is this good?" and "Does this suck?" "The two questions," Barry says, "find everyone."

The moment I decided I would apply for MFA programs for my sabbatical, I became seized with the all-too-familiar doubt about my writing abilities. With my completed triptychs, I was in a slightly better position than when I'd applied to UC Davis a decade earlier, but my static ideas about "talent" fueled my insecurities. I viewed the world of talent as divided into the haves and the have-nots. As much as people offered perspective with comments such as "Of course, the selection process *has* to be rather subjective," part of me believed that one was either talented or not, and that talent was as obvious and tangible as trees and mountains. It didn't really occur to me that talent, or a germ of talent, was just a starting place, that it could be fostered or not. Or that, in fact, the very point of participating in a writing program was to *improve* as a writer. Was my work good? Did it suck? To me, it was one or the other, and I had to wait to find out the answer.

When JoJo died, my husband, Kevin, Natalie, and I drove out to California to meet up with family to clean out her house. While Kevin drove, I studied for the GRE (yeah, I thought I'd take it seriously this time). I would soon apply to MFA programs, most of which still required one to take the GRE. As we drove through the wasteland of Nevada and the irrigated green of California's Central Valley, I tried to drill myself with flash cards but soon grew restless. I stared out the window and the movie of JoJo and me played out: I remembered the weekends at her house, making art, drinking black cherry sodas, singing along to "King of the Road." I thought of how in her presence I grew visible, like a Polaroid picture coming to life. Indeed, JoJo had been the person who'd insisted one afternoon in the spring of 1969 that I not lose sight of myself.

My fall from the grace and nirvana of early childhood came in elementary school. In the cocoon of my girl family—as lopsided as it was with my divorced mom and no dad or male relatives in sight—I was fine, the family baby of whom little was expected. Show up. Be cute. That was plenty. As a result of divorces and the age gap between siblings, I lived mostly as an only child. With no one to measure myself against, it never occurred to me to measure at all.

But once I hit the real world, all my failings came sharply

into focus, and starting on the first day of kindergarten I saw myself anew. Within the first few hours of the school year, we were asked to recite the alphabet, which the other kids must have learned from doting parents. I found myself in my first act of fakery as I moved my mouth in silence while other kids belted out, "A, B, C . . . !" My new self-image was something like the *Peanuts* character Pigpen, a child caught in the center of a swirling cloud of dirt. School was about *doing*, and all the things we did were either right or wrong. Write the alphabet. Recite the alphabet. Say your numbers. Now in Spanish. At recess: Catch the ball, throw the ball, defend yourself. Whatever the task, I felt that I was not doing it right or as well as other kids, and each day, each week, each school year, that feeling of incompetency was seared into me more deeply. Anxious erasing ripped apart my math worksheets. The ball flew past me as I stood with eyes scrunched closed. I fell off the curb watching the girl with the perfect braids fly down the street on her purple mustang. Other kids possessed essential knowledge that eluded me. I was so behind, I'd never catch up.

In the third grade a letter arrived stating that I'd been placed in the class for gifted children. Thus began my first case of impostor syndrome. I knew a mistake had been made, and once I was in the class messing up, I would be swiftly placed back with the commoners. One of the girls in the new class—I will call her Kimberly, for at her essence she *was* a Kimberly—had long been the object of my competency envy. And of all the things she could do—keep the objects under her desk lid looking fresh and organized all year, swing across the monkey bars like a real monkey—I envied Kimberly the most for her painting.

In this world in which competencies were measured and evaluated, I suddenly realized that art was something that could be compared. I'd once drawn and painted with abandon at JoJo's, but now I knew that some art was *better* than others. I knew with certainty that Kimberly's art was better than mine. Original images and bold colors filled her paintings. She always seemed to have a plan, a subject in mind—a valley village, a symmetrical family of four—that seemed important and was nothing that would've ever occurred to me to paint. The subjects of my paintings were solely determined by which paintbrush I happened to pick up first. Pink = heart. Green = grass or, in season, perhaps a Christmas tree. Although no one had ever said so, I *knew* that each of my paintings possessed a fatal flaw, a flaw not always locatable but still inevitable and indisputable.

On one particular day, we were standing as usual before our easels in our blue vinyl aprons, our white papers clothes-pegged to the easels, our wells of green, red, yellow, blue, and black lining their troughs. Suddenly, a golden butterfly appeared on Kimberly's white paper, and inside each wing concentric lines mirrored the wing's perimeter, the lines of pink, orange, and yellow growing closer together until they finally closed in on the center of the wing: a slender flame of fire-engine red.

We were just miles from the epicenter of the Summer of Love, and butterflies, toadstools, and lackadaisical daisy chains were everywhere. But Kimberly's butterfly seemed especially hip because of the genius addition of the concentric lines that were also very much a part of our Electric Kool-Aid Acid Test California. At eight years old, she had her finger on the pulse of the culture. And I wanted that finger to be mine. If my fairy godmother had landed in the classroom at that moment and asked, "Would you like to trade places with Kimberly? Would you like to *become* Kimberly?" I would've said, "Do it."

The next weekend I was at JoJo's again. She'd just come back from visiting my dad on his ranch in Mexico and had brought back a bunch of powdered dyes now stored in squat Gerber baby food jars that lined the shelves of her studio, the Spanish names of the colors announced in JoJo's block draftsman printing on a strip of masking tape across each jar: *AZUL, ROSA, NARANJA, VERDE,* the colors all the more intoxicating translated into Spanish. I felt a thrill thinking about how much potential was locked into each jar.

As the hot wax streaked across my sheet canvas, I felt an unfamiliar feeling of confidence in my design that day. I was eager to see JoJo's reaction as I boldly pulled the brush up, up, and up, forming the arch of the wings, and then tightening and tightening in concentric lines within the wing. We talked of other things as we worked, letting the wax cool and then removing the sheets from their frames and plunging them into the magical buckets of *rosa* and *azul.* And finally our batiks hung on the clothesline, pulsing in the breeze, as JoJo and I took our break on her back steps. She smoked her usual Pall Mall, letting her mouth hang open to let out a gust of smoke, as she stared at our batiks. I waited for her to say something, but she didn't, so finally I asked, "So do you like it?" pointing at my ultra-hip butterfly with its devil-may-care antennae.

"It's okay," she said flatly.

"Oh," I said. I hung my head and began to watch a trail of ants marching along a crack in the cement stairs.

Finally, she added: "It doesn't look like you."

I froze: How could she *know*? The silence rose between us until finally I said in a small voice, "I sort of got the idea from this girl at school."

"That explains it. Didn't think it looked like something you'd come up with."

"I know. This is much better than my pictures," I said, a hot mix of shame and defeat brewing inside me.

JoJo shrugged. "I like your pictures. This is sort of ordinary."

"That's a *great* design!" I said, annoyed.

"I liked that cat you did last time."

I cringed inside, thinking of the cat with the stupid grin and huge triangular ears.

"Ugh!" I said. "That cat is stupid! I hate that cat!"

"Well," she said, stubbing out her cigarette, "you're wrong. That cat has the real you in it. And you're gonna have to get used to the real you."

Our magical weekends together ended after I was ten and moved to Canada, when my mother married my stepfather. JoJo never came to visit, which made sense—my mom was marrying far away from her family—but still I missed her. And then when I was sixteen, my girlfriend Cate and I came down and stayed in her guest room for a week, and she let us do whatever we wanted, including drink her Ernest & Julio Gallo rosé and smoke packs of Virginia Slims cigarettes. Eventually, I saw her at least once a year once I was out on my own, passing through California on the way to somewhere else or on the way back, until my dad's funeral when I was twenty-five.

It was six months after the funeral that I moved to California with my half-baked graduate school plan. This was the first time there was a true falling-out between JoJo and me. A family friend had told her I'd said that I was mad because my dad had left my siblings ten thousand dollars and me only five. She was so mad at me she wouldn't talk to me, though I'd just moved to the area and knew almost no one. The oddest part of all this was that I probably *should* have been annoyed that I'd been so obviously designated as less important than my siblings by my father, but I wasn't. I was grateful to get *anything*.

But now I'm pretty sure I understand what was happening with JoJo. She was grieving for her son, her only child, like crazy. At his funeral she'd told me that she wouldn't miss him because she'd always have her memories of him; I naively took that as fact. It didn't occur to me it was just her denial talking. Another thing I know now that I didn't know then: Grief can make us really, really angry. Still, we'd pretty much patched things up— read: swept them under the rug—by the time I started the grad program at San Francisco State. After that I started coming down to her house routinely for Sunday night dinner, sitting at the same picnic table where we'd so often eaten vanilla ice cream and played War.

I was maybe a smidge snobby then. I wore lots of black. I dyed my hair black. I was perpetually pale and wore lots of red lipstick, knocking myself out playing the role of budding deconstructionist. Nothing in my inner nature is suited toward the existential, the theoretical, the very French. Drilling down to my core, we're going to find Barbra Streisand circa *Funny Girl*. Or maybe Liza Minnelli circa *New York, New York* or even John Travolta circa *Look Who's Talking Too* and a deep desire to be a contestant on *Project Runway*. To be a French deconstructionist, I had to work day and night to fight off my true self.

It wasn't that I set out to be a fraud; it just seemed that my very life depended on it. Not getting into that one MFA program and having, as far as I could see, one single skill (other than waitressing, which isn't so much a skill as the revenue-generating arm of my inner codependent)—the ability to read and then speak about what I'd read—my fate was cast in academia. I was twenty-six. If this didn't work out, I could very likely die without a profession.

But as we morph before their eyes from the people they love into strangers, people who've known us since before we could hold a crayon really have no choice but to stand by—perhaps with gritted teeth. And thus was JoJo's lot. During our dinners, if she asked me to explain structuralism, post-structuralism, or any other sort of ism, I'd impatiently sigh the sigh of the person who is unable to explain what she insists she understands. I remember once spotting a book on her bookshelf entitled *Writing a Poem* and letting out a snort, saying to JoJo, "Kind of simplistic, right?" She looked back at me blankly and then looked away without saying a word. Another time we were driving in my car toward Lake County and I was listening to a particularly garbled jazz singer; when JoJo asked that we change it, I insisted that I didn't understand why, even though I did. Even though I would've no doubt preferred to listen to the soundtrack from *Footloose*.

As luck would have it, not long before this, JoJo discovered writing. Not literary criticism but *creative* writing. She got herself an Apple computer. She was taking a writing class at the senior center. "Oh, how nice for you," I must have said, as if she were doing needlepoint. Can we say "jealous"?

But it wasn't needlepoint, and she didn't give up. While I was agonizing over twenty-page seminar papers stuffed with theory, she was writing four-hundred-page novel after four-hundred-page novel. In fact, she wrote four of these books in a row, looking up every once in a while to say something like "I don't even know what people mean when they talk about 'writer's block.'" The first one she asked me to read—*Ginger Harper*—was about a plucky young redhead who traveled alone to Carson City, Nevada, during the Gold Rush to work as a saloon waitress. A break from literary theory if there ever was one.

So here's the thing. And this is between us, understand?

Ginger Harper wasn't that good.

And—this goes *nowhere*—neither were any of the others.

But JoJo's dream was to be published. She sent them out and out and out and they came back and back and back. And she railed against the publishing industry and I nodded sympathetically, but it wasn't the nod of the outraged. It was the nod of someone for whom it was clear why the manuscripts had come back.

I read each of the books one by one, and even though I was an intolerant poser, I could still discern the difference between the work of my new posturing brain and my untrained responses. I knew that my assessment of these books wasn't merely a by-product of the academic circus in which I routinely cameoed as the ball-bouncing seal. I knew in my core self—the self who liked pop music and wouldn't mind the occasional afternoon at a mall—that these manuscripts would not be published.

I lived alone with the awful knowledge that JoJo's dream would not come true. The books were not publishable because they were full of clichéd dialogue and flat characters but mostly, because they belonged to genres that didn't exist. They were romances minus the bodice ripping; Westerns without ambushes; adventures without, well, real adventure. She knew that I knew the fate of these manuscripts, but we never spoke of it. Whether out of kindness or cowardice, I had kept silent, and now she was gone.

When Kevin, Natalie, and I arrived in the Bay Area, we met up with my family at JoJo's pink bungalow. For days we sorted through her things. Even though she'd lived simply, a zillion decisions still lay before us. For example: the box of pencils—mostly one to three inches long—that she kept to get just a little more use out of? Keep—too awful to toss. Decades of paintings, sketches, mosaics, weavings, and silkscreens? Keep! Definitely keep!

And so it went, and then my sister Kathy called out to me from the drafting room (a lot went on in that room, but it was forever called "the drafting room"), saying, "You need to decide this one."

And there they were, the dead bodies: the unpublished manuscripts. All four of them.

It was hope itself, in white stacks secured with elastic bands.

I lifted one: *Ginger Harper*. Oh, *Ginger Harper*. Yes, I remember you.

I thumbed through a few pages, confirming once again that, yes, this book wasn't very good. My super-talented grandmother, who could spin wool into rugs and a bedtime story that lasted an hour, had spent countless hours of her life writing a book that was mediocre. But how much, I began to wonder, did that matter? I, too, had written and would continue to write stuff that wasn't very good. In fact, I realized standing there, producing mediocre work was an inevitable part of the process of learning to write, and if I were ever going to arrive at my "real writing," I had to accept that I'd be producing pages upon pages that weren't brilliant or shiny or indicative of what maybe, if I kept at it, I might be able one day to do. Suddenly it seemed clear that the answer to the question "Do I suck?" would sometimes be yes. There was no getting around it.

With *Ginger* lying limp in my arms, I remembered how happy JoJo had been when she was writing, how excited she'd been to get her computer with the dot-matrix printer. She kept an old batiked sheet over the monitor to protect it as only people of a certain age are wont to do. She'd spent her time writing because she *liked* writing. It was as simple and as genius as that. She liked writing just as she had liked painting, weaving, gardening, and making batiks. She might have excelled more and gained recognition in those other mediums, but her pleasure had been equal. When she spoke of her writing class, she lit up. Writing at home on her early-model Apple, days would fly by. Though she would've loved to have published her work, she never regretted

THEO PAULINE NESTOR

the time writing took. She never regretted it because we never do regret happiness; we just often seem to avoid it.

I knew I could not toss these manuscripts. They still had value. They were a testament to effort, to spending our time well, to trying our hands at whatever we choose—even the things we're not so good at, even at our work that might never end up finding a home in the world. Mostly, though, I kept them because I wanted to remember the distance she'd covered for me, how she'd made my road to becoming a writer just that much shorter. And because in those flawed pages, I could see some of the real her.

104

1. Not long ago, I went with a couple friends to a creativity con-
    ference in Palm Desert. I was a little nervous, imagining at-
    tendance there might render me a woman who wears strictly
    caftans and lives with multiple cats. But it was actually pretty
    amazing. One of the sessions was led by a group called Play-
    back Theatre, a troupe of improv actors who spontaneously
    acted out stories from the audience; in this case all the stories
    were creativity stories—stories from our lives that affected
    how we see ourselves as creative people. Some people told
    stories of empowerment; others told stories of times they'd
    been discouraged, and each time the troupe would quickly
    huddle together and then act out not an exact interpretation
    of the story but a metaphorical one.

    When my turn came, I told the story of Kimberly, the but-
    terfly with the concentric wings, and how JoJo insisted that I see
    the worth of my own work. In the acted-out version, an actor
    played my narrator as a child who wanted to become a dancer.
    Seeing my story acted out made me realize the importance of
    the story and the importance of our origins as creative people.
    Each of us carries a few seminal stories of our creative history,
    and retelling these stories—and, in some cases, taking note of
    how the stories are limiting—can free us up to be more creative.

    For this exercise, first brainstorm a list of important mo-
    ments or scenes in your history as a creative person. Pick one
    and write it as a story.

2. Pick more stories from the list and write them as stories. As you're writing these stories, think about the limiting beliefs you've had about your own creativity and about creativity in general. And, yes, you do have some. Many of us who loved art in elementary school would never consider sitting down with a pack of crayons now and just having fun. Many of us are sure we're "not good at all" at all sorts of things that we just haven't spent time doing. These beliefs discourage us from pursuing activities we could potentially find pleasurable.

3. Write on this question: What activities make you happy? Do you ever avoid doing those activities, and if so, why?

4. Read Julia and Elizabeth Cameron's book *How to Avoid Making Art (or Anything Else You Enjoy)*.

5. Start asking others for stories from their past about their relationship with their creativity.

6. Consider writing a longer project, a creativity memoir that follows your development as a writer or as an artist in another genre or in a number of genres.

7. Write about a person who has inspired you to create.

8. Write about something that is mediocre or obviously flawed but you still value.

7

The Waiting:
The Hardest Part

Like it or not, the writing life involves a great deal of waiting. You write, you send out, and then you wait. I wish I'd known that earlier. I wish I didn't have to wait to find that out. I wish I were a person who is good at waiting. I wish I were a well-adjusted person who can just attend to whatever is happening right in front of me, a lifeguard with her attention trained to the task at hand. I wish I weren't a person who keeps checking her e-mail to see if she's heard back from the agent, the magazine, the contest. But I take comfort in the fact that I'm in good company. Most writers are totally strung out on the wait. Ideally, we'd put our bid in and then forget about it. I've certainly seen that advice for writers in numerous places: After you submit somewhere, just get on with the next writing project. Obviously, this would be the ideal. Obviously, I'm nowhere close to being that person. I'm prone to obsessing, and writing has provided much fodder for obsessing. Saves me from chewing on my own arm, I guess.

A week or so after I finished Terry Tempest Williams's faculty development seminar, I drove to the post office and dropped down the chute the manila envelopes stuffed with my two fiction writing program applications. Doubling the scope of my admission pool since my first attempt at this ten years earlier, I applied to San Diego State University and the University of Washington in Seattle, choosing two places Kevin and I had family nearby.

Most of us don't want to wait for anything, no matter how benign—dinner, our turn in line at the bank—but waiting takes on a new dimension when one is hoping to be chosen for something one truly and completely wants. With one vulnerable arm stretched in the air, we wait as our second-grade teacher selects the lucky one who'll help pass out the cupcakes, knowing it's impossible to hide our hungry need to be chosen.

To be chosen. *Chosen.* We all want to be picked for the scholarship, or for the coveted job, or by the beautiful person to love us. But for some of us the need to be chosen is more acute. Childhood neglect, the unfulfilled need to be the star of our parents' lives, can render us particularly vulnerable to the high-voltage joy the shortlist can spark. When we're finally picked, we're cartwheeling with excitement. Conversely, not being singled out for love, prizes, or the role of Maria, Dorothy, or Juliet can usher in a flood of anguish, our suspicion confirmed once again that we lack that *je ne sais quoi* of the chosen.

My stepfather, Bill, who entered my life when I was ten, assuaged some of my childhood need to be chosen. He had no obligation to play the part of my dad, but once he signed up for it, he embraced that role and never treated me as if I were any less than fully his own. I'm unfamiliar with the experience of the biological father who stays by you, though I assume it's fabulous in an expected way like breathing oxygen and that those accustomed to paternal stability sleep eight uninterrupted hours a night and whiz through standardized tests. I do know, however, the particular and exquisite happiness of someone *choosing* to parent you, of having someone show up for you when they could've easily chosen not to. Even without biology and society's mandate, Bill cared for me when I had the flu, attended my back-to-school nights, and figured out how to get me home from Montreal during an airline strike.

I'd called Bill "Dad" since a few days after he and my mother got married in 1971. Some may think I rushed in on the rebound, but I knew right away he was the real deal. And even though for years I always felt like I had to say no to the question "But is he your *real* dad?" for me the true answer always felt like yes. He was the dad who taught me to ski, who watched *The Twilight Zone* with me on rainy Saturday afternoons, who stood up for me and believed in me. My biological father was the one who seemed anything but real. He was the check in the mail, the card at Christmas, the awkward hug, the Dad of Ninth Step amends that came too late to take root, JoJo's son now long passed away from cancer.

Even after he and my mother divorced, my dad and I managed to hang on to each other. It was just one more adjustment for a family slightly off course from the ideal, but I'd been making these adjustments my whole life, ever since my parents broke up when I was one year old.

Right around the time Natalie was born, Bill started to get sick. His smoking-related coughing worsened, and eventually he was diagnosed with emphysema. When he played Duck, Duck, Goose with Natalie, he'd get winded after a few minutes and would tell her with discernible shame that she'd "won." During a Christmas visit, he was hospitalized for pneumonia. In February, he and his new wife (wife number four, but when we love people, we try not to do too much counting) came for a month-long stay, and by then his emphysema had severely limited his ability to move around. We had to call the paramedics more than once when he went into respiratory failure. But I couldn't recognize his decline; I refused to accept it. I was not prepared to lose him, the person I figured might fend off lions and tigers and bears if such animals were to come after me.

On the last day of March of 1997, the director of the University of Washington's English Creative Writing Program called to tell me I was the first person on the waiting list for the next year's fiction group. And this is good news *because* . . . ? They had eight slots, which had all been offered to their top choices (uh-*hunh*); but if any of those candidates were to decide not to come, there could be a spot open. "If it were offered," he asked, "would you take it?"

Yes . . . yes, I would. Not only was the school my first choice, but I'd be close enough to go back and forth between Seattle and my dad's place on Vancouver Island. I had to get in.

The waiting began.

Three weeks later the English Creative Writing Program director finally called me back. I was in! The suspense was over. Something in that thin ten-page writing sample had secured me a spot after all. I've had a few truly sweet writing victories since then, but this was the first time I felt my promise as a writer confirmed, and I was silly with joy, thrilled that in just a few months I'd be nestled into the program and writing.

I couldn't wait to tell my dad. I knew he'd be so happy for me.

"I have news!" I said into the phone, looking out at the red and white canyons across the lava field, the colors suddenly Technicolor bright.

"I do too, I'm afraid," he said.

My heart dropped. "Okay, you first," I said, starting to feel dizzy.

"The doctor says I have lung cancer."

The world went black. I know we fumbled through a conversation about the X-rays, what the doctor had said, what it all meant. But all I remember is clenching the phone like a life preserver, thinking, I'm losing him. My protector.

We were about to hang up when he said, "Wait. What's your news?"

"Oh, I got in," I whispered.

"What?"

"The MFA program in Seattle. I got in." It seemed so trivial now.

"That's terrific!" he said, happy for me, although I no longer cared.

I barely remember saying good-bye and hanging up. What I remember is sitting down on the floor, staring at the weave of the rug, trying to figure out how things come together and fall apart so quickly, trying to remember how to stand and how to speak.

On June 11 we moved to Seattle, and on July 17 my dad died. In the five weeks in between my body was on the freeway or on the ferry and my spirit was circling the territory in between Seattle and his Vancouver Island town like a hawk that's forgotten where home is. Natalie was two, and she came along with me most of the time. For the last few weeks of his life, Bill stayed at the hospital on the palliative care floor. I found out what the word "palliative" means and wished I hadn't. Whenever I'd go to visit him, he'd be in the middle of a book: one time, *Angela's Ashes*, the next a history of London. "I don't know why," he said, holding up the thick book, "but I'm still so curious about everything."

His room was always crowded with visitors—my brother's family, my dad's wife, Natalie and me. Once he cleared everyone out of the room and asked me to stay.

"You have made me very happy," he said. I'm ashamed to say that I wanted more. What could be more than making someone happy? For some insane reason I wanted him to say that he was proud of me, but he didn't. Of course, to him nothing was better than happiness and I didn't ask for anything more. I took the gift of "happy" and held it as tightly as I could, hoping that might reverse the effects of decades of smoking, but it didn't. The next week he was gone.

I felt guilty that I hadn't done something spectacular with my life before he died. I wanted to prove to him that everything he'd invested in me had been worthwhile, that I hadn't taken anything for granted. Perhaps one of the differences between being raised by your "real" father and a stepfather is that no matter how exquisite the love and the care, I still felt like I needed to repay, to prove. Or maybe that's just exactly what it feels like when your dad dies too soon.

The rest of that summer passed slowly. I waited for grief to end and for new beginnings. I longed for the fall to come, for Natalie's preschool to start up, and for my first quarter in the MFA program to begin. Slowly the days of a hot August slipped by and September arrived with its new beginning: My dream of attending writing school began, just a few days after I found out I was expecting baby number two.

1. Make a list of times when you had to wait for something you really wanted or to find out bad or good news. Write about one of them.

2. Now write about another.

3. Write about what those two times had in common and how they differed.

4. Write about a time when you got what you wanted. Was it all that you wished for, or was getting what you'd desired a mixed blessing?

5. Write about a time when you didn't get what you wanted. Was it all bad? Was there some advantage you can see now to not getting what you'd wanted? Could you see the silver lining even then?

6. Write about this topic: "Being Chosen." When have you been one of the "chosen"? What did it feel like to be chosen? What is the dark side of being chosen?

7. Write about a person you chose or a person who chose you.

8

Find Your Tribe; Find Your Voice

Even if you don't know a single writer in real life, you can build your own writing community by staking your claim on the writers who speak to you and inspire you, the writers who excite you about the possibility of writing. I think that very early on each of us knows the type of voice and stories we are drawn to. I've always found myself yearning for a representation of my own experience on the page. As a writer I long to break the isolation of the unarticulated experience, the trap of the ineffable. And as a reader, I am hungry for literary representations of the self. It's not so much that I'm eager to know the details of others' lives or that I believe my own experience is so compelling that they should want to know mine; it's that I adore the wizardry of the alchemical process in which life is spun into story.

In the sixth grade, I had my first flicker of knowledge of who my tribe of writers was, the first flush of my crush on first-person narrative. Two books I read that year that woke in me the desire to tell stories were Judy Blume's *Are You There God? It's Me, Margaret* and Xaviera Hollander's *The Happy Hooker*. The Blume book I found in a bookmobile on a snowy afternoon. I cracked it open right there, and as I dripped melted snow on the linoleum floor, I heard this first-person girl voice that had traveled through the hands of some New York publisher and then into my local library and then up the snowy hill into the bookmobile to save me. I'd just moved to Canada from California the year before, right after my mom and Bill were married. I needed a bit of saving. The narrator of *Are You There God? It's Me, Margaret* was a girl like me, a girl who struggled with friends and who needed to get her first bra. Blume made ordinary sixth-grade life pop open with a *pow*. In the book's pages I heard the voice of someone like me, a friend, not the artificially sweet voice of children's books that described a life sterile with perfection.

The Happy Hooker came through the sixth-grade information pipeline in an old, crinkly lunch bag. It was passed this way—in the ancient way that knowledge is passed—from hand to hand through the sixth grade. No one really knew whose book it was or who'd started the chain, but we all revered the importance of the book, and we were all united by the fact that we had read the same story and we'd all gone to the same lengths to hide it from our parents. Once in a while we'd check in on who had it at the moment and then nod sagely, knowing one more had been added to our numbers. For me, the book was more than an initiation into the adult world of sex, though. It was the *voice* that was so magnetic. I adored the way Xaviera turned to the camera—just as Blume's narrator had—and just told her story. From her ordinary life of johns and tricks, she pulled out a gritty real-life narrative. I didn't know it yet, but I was falling in love with the first person.

Decades later, in my first quarter of my MFA program in Seattle, I couldn't have been more intimidated as a thirty-five-year-old pregnant woman in a room where the average age was twenty-six, the average undergrad alma mater Stanford. When we had to introduce ourselves the first day, I trembled and my voice broke as I said my name. Intimidated not just by the other students and the tall and urbane professor, I was daunted by the fact that my presence in the room announced to the world my intention of becoming a writer. But it *was* my intention and I hoped I was prepared to face the challenge.

One of the first assignments was to share with the class a piece of writing we admired—simple enough, except that it very quickly morphed into a round of Defending Your Life. As we read through each piece, the professor would look straight at the student who brought it in and say, "So? What's so great about this?" That's the thing about love. It's very hard to defend. When you're the student, though, you really only have two choices: losing face in front of your peers by not going up to bat, or going up to bat and maybe striking out. So up we all went, one by one. One guy had brought in a restaurant review. In answer to the What-do-you-like-about-it? question, he spat out that he liked the tone of the review, the voice of the writer. The professor looked aghast, made a sort of scoffing sound, and said, "Are you serious? This is the most ordinary sort of journalism I can imagine." We all swallowed, our own turns just a few beats away.

I barely survived my defense of an Alice Munro story, taking a hit for having a "solipsistic aesthetic," as I'd said that I enjoyed Munro partly because she's a Canadian woman. Most of us got through somehow with just minor cuts and bruises, until it came to . . . I'll call her Minnie. Minnie had brought in a pretty decent poem. I can't remember it completely, maybe because my memory is blacked out by what happened next, but I remember it was something about a bird and I thought, Yeah, I can see liking this. After she finished reading the poem, the professor started his usual round of questioning. Instead of rallying and trying to swat at the ball, Minnie kept saying stuff like "I don't know" and "I'm not sure." The temperature in the room rose. Throats cleared. We shot looks of encouragement Minnie's way.

Finally, Tall and Urbane just asked point blank: "*Why*, then, did you bring it in?"

Minnie spilled the whole truth and it wasn't pretty: The truth was she'd looked through pages and pages of stuff and nothing—how surprising?—seemed good enough. Finally, she remembered a poem that one of her undergrad professors had swooned over. He'd been very convincing that this poem was of tremendous merit and she'd reasoned that if he thought it that good, surely it must be, and so she decided that's what she would bring.

Stunned silence flooded the room. Our eyes darted from Minnie to Tall and Urbane and back to Minnie.

"Okay," he said, "I understand why you did this. But this won't work. It's better to bring in something that everyone else hates but that you truly love than to bring someone else's pick. You have to *know* what writing you love. You just *have* to."

After we'd all taken our turns, he shared with us all the low-brow and highbrow writers he loved and what they meant to him. The list did not include the usual suspects such as Faulkner and Shakespeare. The list did include Mary Gaitskill and *Sein-feld*, which excited me beyond measure. He concluded by saying that even though these writers might not be on other people's lists, he would go down defending them.

In that moment and throughout the quarter, I felt his love for *his* writers. He was a true fan, and his excitement for his writers was contagious. His enthusiasm encouraged me to claim the writers I loved as my own and to carry them with me, to allow them to nurture me as a writer. I slowly came to understand what the professor had been up to in those sweaty tribunals. He'd been forcing us to defend our people, to gather our own tribe around us. He knew we'd need their voices to find our own.

I already knew what I liked in writing—in a way, I'd known it since the sixth grade when I'd read Blume and Hollander—but what I hadn't been able to do before this was to *own* what I liked, to not feel shame that it wasn't highbrow enough or not avant garde. Suddenly it was okay that I wasn't cool enough to like DeLillo or Pynchon.

It was kind of like when I was in high school, and I felt this shiver of shame when a new friend would flip though my record collection—a seventies rite of friendship, to be sure. There were cool-kid (read cool-boy) sanctioned albums that you were supposed to have—*Led Zeppelin I, II, III,* and *IV* pop instantly to mind. And then there was my collection, which ranged from my first purchase (*The Divine Miss M*) to something more recent, like the soundtrack to *American Graffiti.* I didn't like Led Zeppelin or any of the other cool-boy music. At all. Sure, I might have slow danced in the basement of the United Church to "Stairway to Heaven," but that music never spoke to me. What was it about, anyway? "There's a lady who's sure all that glitters is gold." Even then—years before reading about what Gloria Steinem called "the click" you get when you realize something you've always taken for normal is, in fact, horrifically sexist—I felt a pre-feminist twinge whenever I heard Zeppelin. Maybe it had everything to do with my early and unrelenting distaste for the word "lady."

Anyway, my new friend would soon flip past my safety albums kept at the front: David Bowie's *ChangesOneBowie* and Supertramp's *Crime of the Century,* and it wouldn't take long before she got into the really embarrassing stuff that I deeply and truly loved. We're talking Cher's *Gypsies, Tramps & Thieves,* folks. The Supremes. Al Stewart's *The Year of the Cat,* an album I'd secretly memorized, which I swore held within it the secrets to all of adulthood. Joni Mitchell, absolutely. The Beach Boys, check. And yes, Billy Joel.

Similarly, I felt that My Writers revealed my questionable taste, my rudimentary reading skills, my lack of intellect, my poor breeding, my ADD, my general lack of savoir faire. But whatever they might've shown about me that I feared, I also loved them fiercely and hated to risk exposing them to criticism. If someone were to say something untoward about Nora Ephron, for example, it would feel as if the family name was at stake. These were the writers who were giving me permission to be myself. And however low my self-esteem might have been at times, there was always a part of me that quietly rooted for the triumph of my goofy spirit.

And that part of me was a reader. Before anyone becomes a writer, she is a reader. She may not be an avid reader, but she's read some writers as if her life depended upon them. Because it has.

The writers who speak to us, who send out the siren call and lure us to bring pen to paper, are the ones who have revealed a view of the world that makes sense to us—and that view of the world is often very different from the dominant view among the people who surround us, the people who've taught us what life is and who we can be in the world. Sometimes, the examples are extreme.

A friend of mine, Carlene Cross, wrote a book called *Fleeing Fundamentalism: A Minister's Wife Examines Faith* chronicling her experience as a young woman falling into Christian Fundamentalism and falling for a young, charismatic minister, then crawling her way out of Fundamentalism when she discovered her husband's dark, secret life and realized that Fundamentalism was annihilating her spirit. After Carlene visited my memoir class one quarter, a student in the class who'd grown up a Fundamentalist mailed Carlene's book to a woman in a similar situation. He described to me how much hope the book had given this woman, how she'd kept it hidden and then read it when no one was around, how it felt like a lifeline out of a hopeless situation.

Sometimes it's subtler, the need for the book seemingly less urgent, but the essence of the situation is the same: The beloved book is somehow allowing you to believe that the way you see life is valuable and the way you want to express yourself is possible. The book is calling you to something.

Right before my twenty-second birthday, back when I was waiting tables in Santa Fe, a friend whom I'd met in a creative writing class my freshman year came to visit. As she was leaving, she handed me a copy of Nora Ephron's *Heartburn*. "You're going to *love* this," she said.

I spent the day with the book where love often lands us: in bed. I read all of *Heartburn* that day, pausing routinely to examine the front and back covers and the author's name, as if that might give me further entrance into her first-person world. Written as a novel, the book is basically a roman à clef, pretty much an exact account of Ephron's divorce from Carl Bernstein of Woodward and Bernstein fame. The names and some details were changed. But the sense that you're reading an actual account—a funny, heart-searing account—of the author's own experience is visceral.

It was more than her sincerity that won my heart, though. Because I'm, in fact, not a huge fan of the strictly confessional; if a book is described as "heartfelt," I tend to steer clear. The writers in my tribe mix it up. They go a bit crazy with form. Their writing sings with their original and quirky voices. They've got big-"*P*" Personality on the page. And in Ephron's *Heartburn*, I divined that; I couldn't name it yet. It was more like *grunt me like this grunt. Me want to do this grunt.* Now I can pick up *Heartburn* and locate and name what thrilled me then and what thrills me now. First, Nora dropped recipes right into the story. *Heart-*

burn was published in 1983! The word "foodie" wouldn't make it into popular vernacular for decades. These are the John Updike and Raymond Carver years, years of show-don't-tell fiction. Who dropped recipes into fiction back then? Nora. Nora alone.

The other *it* quality of *Heartburn* for me: the way Ephron is just turning right to us—she knows we're there, she's addressing us—and telling us about her life, her dad, her therapy, her broken heart, her cheating second husband, her neurotic first husband.

And here's the feminist moment (if that scares you, be scared or skip to the next chapter): The life she's telling us about is *a woman's life*. If I follow the bread crumbs of the voices that have spoken to me and especially those who spoke to me when I was young (the years when my schools assigned me to read exactly zero female writers), it becomes clear that I was looking to find my own experience articulated in a culture in which female experience rarely made it into the public consciousness—in print, on the small screen, or on the big screen. I wanted to understand my own experience, and I wanted to know that it was worthy of articulating, of being made into literature, that my desires and fears could be the arc a story climbs and falls on. The bread crumbs tell the story: Nora Ephron, Patti Smith, Joni Mitchell, the Supremes, Mary Tyler Moore, Judy Blume, and Xaviera Hollander. Girls like me.

The writers of your tribe will be the writers you love and the writers who somehow hold a space open for you in the world, like a tent flap for you to slip under. Because they've cleared the trail ahead—even just a little—you feel like you can go ahead and say what you want to say the way you want to say it. Sometimes these people are in our tribe because we share a commonality like gender or race: You both belong to a subset whose experience isn't part of the dominant paradigm. James Baldwin credited Richard Wright with holding the flap up for him, giving him the nod of acknowledgment with his title *Notes of a Native Son*. Alice Walker credits Zora Neale Hurston as a writer a generation before her who wrote about rural African-Americans, clearing the way for her to write *The Color Purple*.

Sometimes we need a writer ahead of us to remind us that our experience counts, even if that experience is one that is rarely portrayed in literature, film, or song. A former student of mine, Tim Elhajj, who grew up in a small town in Pennsylvania, remembers reading Tobias Wolff's *This Boy's Life* and being inspired by his ordinary characters. "These weren't highfalutin people," Tim says. "They were getting themselves into trouble, stealing stuff." Reading *This Boy's Life* in college helped pave Tim's way years later when he sat down to write his memoir about his slow climb through recovery from a heroin addiction, *Dopefiend: A Father's Journey from Addiction to Redemption*.

In other cases, it's another artist's relationship to their subject matter that allows you to find your own stories and your voice in which to tell those stories. In the documentary *Joni Mitchell: Woman of Heart and Mind*, Joni Mitchell talks about the way Bob Dylan cleared the path for her:

> Bob Dylan inspired me with the idea of the personal narrative.
> He would speak as if to one person in a song, you know, like,

"You've got a lot of nerve to say you are my friend." Nobody had ever written anything like that in song form, you know? Such a personal, strong statement, and his influence was to personalize my work. "I feel this *for* you, *from* you, or *because* of you." That was the key. Okay, this opens all the doors. Now we can write about anything.

Mitchell's album *Blue* is a great example of how those doors did, in fact, open for Mitchell. *Blue* is Mitchell's very original work inspired by Dylan, filled with personal narratives that demonstrate how the universal experience can reside in the first person singular. When she talks about the last time she saw Richard in '68, I feel like I surely must know Richard—or at least someone very much like him.

Mitchell was a writer I early identified as a teacher, years before I knew I wanted to write. Flipping through the albums at my regular babysitting gig at fourteen, I stumbled upon *Court and Spark*. I played that album the entire summer (probably driving the toddler in my charge half mad—sorry!), memorizing the thing whole, my mind relentlessly trying to understand the magic of lines about "the red, red rogue" who cooked "good omelettes and stews" and partygoers with passport smiles. Joni had been to that party, I knew that. She went to a party and then wrote about it. I went to parties. Could I write about them? A simple question was planted, though it would take years to answer. (By the way, it might be worth stating here that during that phase in which I was memorizing albums whole, I was rightly considered an entirely mediocre student at my high school, where I held a C average—my "gifted" days long behind me.)

Sometimes, it's a writer's approach to form and structure that speaks to you. When I saw Nora drop recipes into her narrative, something in me lit up, a feeling of possibility, an excitement for telling a story in a way that draws attention to the storytelling. The first time I felt blown away by a writer's approach to structure was when I was sixteen and I went to see *Annie Hall* with my engineering-student boyfriend. As we left the theater, I turned to him, ecstatic, and said, "Oh my God, what did you think?"

"It was okay," he said.

"'Okay'?" I said. "*What?* It's genius. It's the best movie I've ever seen. The split screens! The subtitles! The way they go back in time to his childhood classroom?"

To him the movie was strange, chaotic, but for me the movie was life altering. It was the first time I felt the electricity of inspiration. I didn't have the means, the knowledge, the skills, or the experience to put this inspiration to work yet, but I felt the roar of possibility of taking an autobiographical story and playing with it; how a fractured form could replicate layers of consciousness; how autobiographical stories could be used as a launchpad for pointing to stuff in the culture. Of course, I couldn't say any of that back then—I can barely put into words what the movie means to me now.

Whether we understand why something excites us creatively doesn't matter; what matters is that we identify what we love and that we gather it near to us. We list the writers, painters, filmmakers, and songwriters we love in a place in our hearts and minds reserved for treasures. Even if everyone we know disagrees with us (and believe me, many have disagreed with me about Woody

Allen), we learn to believe in our own tastes—not as empirically correct but as subjectively correct for us. We become advocates for ourselves and our own creative vision. We stop questioning what we love and allow ourselves to just love. We toss aside the raved-about book everyone else loves that leaves us cold; we return to our own racing hearts, no longer caring how far away we've traveled from the pack. We go to our writers and listen. We prepare ourselves to recognize the sound of our own voices as they begin to lift from the page.

1. Take a big piece of paper (I like the flip charts that have an adhesive strip on the back of each piece) and make a list of your favorite books, writers, poets, songs, songwriters, movies, directors, TV shows, and visual artists. If you tend to forget, go look through your bookshelf and your music collection. Think about when you first got excited about writing: Who were the writers who spoke to you? Think about when you were a teenager and you memorized song lyrics: Whose lyrics were they? Think about the first time you were blown away by a museum exhibit. Take your time with this list. When you're done, write the words "My Tribe" at the top of the paper and hang it in your writing space.

   I hesitate to share with you my tribe because they are *my* tribe, and the point isn't for you to adopt my aesthetic but to realize your own. But sometimes an example is helpful, so here it is:

   "Theo's Tribe" (in no particular order, not even alphabetical): Lorrie Moore, Alice Munro, Anton Chekhov, Tina Fey, Meghan Daum, Lynda Barry, Amy Krouse Rosenthal, Spalding Gray, Anne Lamott, Kate Braverman, Kathryn Harrison, Sandra Tsing Loh, Geoff Dyer, Terry Tempest Williams, Joni Mitchell, Joe Strummer, Gloria Steinem, Nora Ephron, Patricia Hampl, Mary Karr, Joan Didion, Erma Bombeck, Woody Allen, Amy Benson, Beth Lisick, Vivian Gornick,

Elvis Costello, Lucille Ball, Lauryn Hill, Larry David, Junot Díaz, Art Spiegelman, Bobbie Ann Mason, James Baldwin, Lauren Slater, Jo Ann Beard, Andre Dubus, Margaret Cho, Milan Kundera, Wassily Kandinsky, Mark Rothko, Ellen Forney, Adrienne Rich, Candace Walsh, Tony Hoagland, Cheryl Strayed, Dave Eggers, Mike Daisey, Maxine Hong Kingston, Suzanne Finnamore, E.J. Levy, Alison Bechdel, Steve Almond, Lena Dunham.

2. Invest in purchasing your favorite books. Keep a handful of the books from your inner circle on your writing desk. When you're feeling stuck, read a page or two as a break from writing. Myself, I'm crazy for signed books. It's the one and only thing I've ever collected. My goal is to have a signed copy of each of my favorite books.

3. Pick one of your favorite writers and set out to read all of his or her work. Keep a notebook for your reactions to the work, lines you particularly like, and insights into the characteristics of their writing.

4. Pick a scene or passage from one of your favorite writers and write an imitation of that scene or passage. Using your own content, copy the essence of the passage. If there's a bit of dialogue followed by description followed by an insight, then take your story and create a bit of dialogue followed by a description followed by an insight. It's a challenging assignment that will teach you a great deal about how a writer you so revere is actually pulling it off.

5. Make a playlist of the songs that are important to you as a

writer, that somehow urge you to write and remind you of a point of view that you want to express in your writing.

6. Go on an "artist's date." In Julia Cameron's seminal book on creativity, *The Artist's Way*, she talks about the importance of going on a regularly scheduled "artist's date" by yourself to a location that inspires you. She suggests an array of possibilities, from the ballet to the aquarium to a bookstore, but the location isn't as important as the inspiration that it brings you personally. Her argument is that writers have to keep replenishing their wells of images so that their work does not become dry and stale.

    I had a dual reaction when I first read this idea: Part of me thought, Yeah, right, like I have time to go on an "artist's date," and another part of me was quite thrilled by the fact that I was being given permission to go out and explore the world; that I wouldn't be goofing off from work but doing something productive—replenishing the well. I have yet to establish a routine of the artist's date, but I have done a few more fun and stimulating activities since I first read about this idea, including a trip to the Seattle Asian Art Museum to see a collection of Japanese prints, a long exploration through a record store, and a couple of forays into a high-end fabric shop. What do any of these have to do with writing? Not a whole lot, but when I see the beauty others have created and how others have followed their idea from seed to fruition, I do feel inspired to get to work.

7. Go to bookstore readings and library events. Going to hear

writers read can be a great source of inspiration. I also find at book events that a lot of spontaneous conversations sprout up between people in the audience about books. Check your local library and the bookstore's Web page for news of upcoming events.

9

Permission to Write

Near the end of the first year of the MFA program, it was announced that a Famous-to-the-Well-Read Writer would be the program's visiting writer the next year. I'd heard of him! In fact, I could remember acutely reading an oft-anthologized story of his back in Utah five years earlier. On a blastingly hot summer day free from the demands of teaching, I had lain on our sofa with the air-conditioner pumping out cool air, working my way through a pile of library books.

Famous-to-the-Well-Read's story had been collected into a volume of *Best American Short Stories*. I remembered reading through the collection with a sense of wonder and profound jealousy. I had recently turned thirty, an age when career envy can reach a shrill high C. Everything you were going to do by thirty mocks you, and you really don't get that you're not alone in that. There on my sofa I read his amazing story chock full of literary merit and grit, which had everything I hoped my writing would possess. After finishing the story, I flipped back to the author's bio. He'd been in the Writers' Workshop at the University of Iowa, natch. Like the other writers in the collection, he was a rock star, distant and unreachable. How he'd gotten to where he was as a writer, I'd never know. I'd be more likely to run into David Bowie at our desert town's Smith's Food King.

And now suddenly, five years later, he was coming to my MFA program. He'd be teaching our workshop next year, and in fact, in just a few weeks, he would be visiting our class. Coincidentally (or was it fate?), he'd be coming to our class the very day my story was slated to be workshopped. What's more, our regular instructor thought it would be a great idea for Famous to *lead* our workshop.

If I get very quiet and honest, I call up a memory of my hope that Famous would be blown away by my story. That perhaps with a few deftly delivered pieces of praise he'd raise my group status from middle-of-the-pack to literary star. Later we'd become friends—not quite equals but close—hashing out writing troubles over coffee in crowded Seattle cafés. It is difficult to access that memory now, though, because the events that followed diverged so sharply from that fantasy.

Did he love my story? No. Did he like it even? Nope. Did he think the story worthy of a line-by-line scrutiny? An absolute yes. And so that's how I spent an hour one mid-May afternoon near the end of the millennium: sitting in silence (the writer never talks in workshops, just quietly sits and considers all the sage advice shooting around her like gunfire, occasionally scribbling something thoughtful in her notebook, such as "Fuck off") as Famous carefully explained line by line everything that was wrong with the story. The story was set in San Francisco during the 1989 earthquake, and included a detail about watching the headlights of the cars on the bridge heading north toward Marin County. This detail excited Famous to a point of near-fury.

"If the narrator is in San Francisco and she's watching cars heading north, she'd be looking at *taillights*, not headlights," he announced to the class, as if making his closing argument to a grand jury.

Pregnant with baby number two, I barely held it together, sitting through the next few minutes in that overly warm and crowded classroom. Baby, objecting to the heat and the stress, pounded out her objection with her small feet and then pulled an elbow across my enormous midsection. Shock and anger vied for position, but mostly I burned with shame as my lifelong fear of being inaccurate had just been played out in a public setting. All the other literary crimes committed in the story—lack of action and imagination, bad dialogue, a passive narrator—seemed not so bad compared to the Giant Crime of Inaccuracy, of getting taillights mixed up with headlights. And while the goal of fiction is to make up swaths of life that feel real, I'd offered up, yet again, something real that seemed made up because I couldn't even accurately report what I'd actually seen, a failing that I generally try to keep well hidden. (If an eyewitness to a crime is needed, I am not—*should not be*—your first pick. I don't know whether it's that I'm just spacey or if it's the second-guessing that undoes me, but accuracy in reporting is not my strong suit.)

A full-scale loss of face and dashing of hopes had not been

my plan for the day; in fact, I'd been hoping from Famous for something I shouldn't have even been asking for from anyone else: permission to write. And now saddled with working with Famous for the rest of the MFA program, I'd be spending lots of time in public situations with someone in authority, someone whose work I respected, who didn't "get" me, who didn't like my writing, and who was extremely good at picking it apart. It didn't help that I knew that Famous's criticisms of my work were accurate. My narrators were passive. My stories lacked action and certainly imagination, and sometimes I got details wrong. In short, the moment I'd predicted when I held JoJo's failed manuscript in my hands had arrived. I sucked and people knew it.

Ideally, this story should end up with Famous being just the school of tough love I needed and the best teacher I ever had. It should end with my fiction making a dramatic turn for the better, my characters turning from wimpy to active, my details sharp with accuracy. It doesn't. It ends up with me becoming increasingly down on my writing and increasingly irritated with Famous. It ends up with me learning quite a bit in spite of him and sometimes because of him and then graduating from the program with a shaky sense of my own ability to write fiction.

But there is a good part. Really. The good part came a while after I graduated from the program and saw Famous for perhaps the last time. By then I was mostly a stay-at-home mom and I wrote when I could, taking care of Natalie and her new sister, Jessie, most of the time. No one in the world cared whether I wrote or not. Usually I had an hour a day during nap time to do whatever I wanted, and most days—when I wasn't totally exhausted—I chose to write. My stories were still fictional but gradually becoming memoir. I started to write triptychs again. It was weird that I'd somehow forgotten them during the fiction writing program, but I had. But the triptych had waited for me to come back. I started taking the words that my new life had evolved into—marriage, motherhood, family—and putting them at the center of the page. No matter what I learned in graduate school, I had to keep reminding myself to be myself, to listen to the sound of my own voice.

Almost every new writer yearns for permission to write. Ideally, an established, maybe even famous writer will examine a small sample of your writing and quickly issue a You've-got-it declaration. We imagine that, like the results of a pregnancy test, the answer is binary: yes or no. Thumbs up or down. Positive or negative. Once this permission has been received, your flight will launch, never faltering, never touching down in the Land of Doubt again.

Meanwhile, here on Earth, established writers are flawed, subjective beasts who may be unable, unwilling, or just too tired or busy to issue the permission you crave. They, for whatever reason that may have no bearing on your talent or potential, could *despise* your writing. Let's say, though, that they *do* like your work and they are able and willing to toss you a crumb of approval. It's still not going to satisfy you. The trouble with approval is there's never enough of it. Given approval once, you're not set for life—busily writing and overcoming every obstacle, steadily nurtured by the nod you received ten years ago. No matter how potent, once a shot of approval has faded in your bloodstream, you'll be wanting another one. Sounds decidedly like addiction, doesn't it?

Beyond approval, I've also wanted my instructors' validation that sitting down to write was a worthy use of my time. I wanted permission to stop my endless chain of obligatory tasks. I wanted someone to clear the brush of doubt around me and give me the peace of mind to write.

In Virginia Valian's "Learning to Work," the essay that helped me get through my thesis, she describes her own fear of work and that of others who've shared a common fear of "relinquishing control of oneself: of being a slave, or going into a tomb, being buried alive, being shut off from the world" and that she had to learn that "losing myself in my work was not dangerous." These words hit me as hard today as they did twenty-five years ago when I first read them as a graduate student staring down the abyss of a one-hundred-page thesis. Today the Internet is down in my house. I have no pressing work to do. My kids are off at arts camp and don't need to be picked up for several hours. And adding to the quiet of this day, it is gray and cold even though it is July and many people I know are out of town on summer vacations. This is the day that I've said I've been waiting for: a writing day. And yet, it scares me. There is nothing between me and the page, and that does feel dangerous. I can stand perched above it for a good long while, the same way I can stand on a warm dock above a cool lake, terrified of the moment of contact with the water. Terrified of breaking through the skin of the surface and being in, committed fully to swimming. And yet, I want to swim. Why not just dive in?

Ideally, I'd be pushed in. Stripped of my volition, I'm given the chance to do what I long for. For many writers, a deadline is the push. Someone's waiting for your work; you have to do it. But for much of the work we truly yearn to do, there is no deadline. The only broken promise is the one we made to ourselves.

So here I am, beginning to swim. The guy from the phone company still isn't here to fix the Internet and probably won't be for several hours. I've used all my tricks to coax myself in. A pot of black tea. Background music. Looking over notes for a good while before actually doing the writing. But finally I do get to it, and partly I am here because of my teachers—teachers like Famous—who taught me by the example of their own work that it is safe to be alone with my own thoughts, that I won't be "buried alive" when I give myself over to writing.

My need for someone to tell me that it's okay to write, for me to take the time to sit and follow my own thoughts, seems to be relentless. I thought it would go away once I was in an MFA program, then once I was published in a magazine. After that, I hoped that maybe a published book would do the trick. But whatever writing milestones I hit, the desire for someone to tell me that I can spend the afternoon, the morning, or the week to write is always there.

What does it look like to give permission to ourselves? For me, it's the computer not turned on. The e-mails unanswered. It's sitting in the quiet of a morning punctuated by only a crow's caw and the occasional roar of children's voices from the neighborhood park. Nothing adding to those sounds except the scratch of a pen rhythmically moving across the paper. It's the unanswered phone. It's looking out the window and letting one thought give rise to the next, an endless succession of waves that rise, crest, and fall onto the shore. It's the sound of the calico cat making its ascent to the windowsill. It's knowing that all the other stuff you need to do will get done. Or it won't.

It's the stillness we both crave and repel. It's the knowledge that following our own thoughts is a pastime as important as, or even more important than, following the thoughts of another.

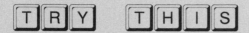

1. When making your schedule for the week, pencil in a time for writing. Ideally, you will be able to pick regular times of the day or a certain day each week, which will allow you to condition yourself that these times are for writing, reinforcing the idea that you are "allowed" to write during these times. Keep in mind, however, that schedules work very well for some people but actually cause some to feel constricted and therefore to work less.

2. List teachers and professors who've played a significant role in your development. Beside their names, jot a note or two about the lessons they taught you, including the inadvertent ones. Pick one teacher and write about what they taught you.

3. Identify your role models for working. Who do you know who seems to have already gotten "permission" to write or do other creative activities? My grandmother, JoJo, never seemed to be waiting for permission to be creative. She supported herself most of her life with her part-time landscape architecture business and the rest of the time she did whatever she pleased. Some of her art was displayed and sold in galleries, but much of her art she did simply for her own enjoyment. When I think of her, I feel this sense of peace and freedom to use my time however I like. Who are your creative role models? Make a list and maybe post it or a picture of these people near your workstation.

4. Answer this: Who has given *you* permission to write?

5. Answer this: How can you give *yourself* permission to write?

10

"The Mother and Child Reunion Is Only a Motion Away"

My second daughter, Jessica, was born near the end of the first year of the MFA program. I brought her bundled in her Baby-Björn carrier to class the next week, and I think that says a lot about me —and it's not all good. Being a mother of now two small children didn't melt away any of my ambitions as a writer or alter or mitigate any of my passions as a person. Whether that's made me a bad or negligent mother, I've frankly stopped wondering, though this question once possessed me. Raised on *Mary Tyler Moore* and cautionary tales such as *A Star Is Born*, I was certain most of my life that family and career were either/or propositions for women. It took me a long time to decide to become a mother, and I'm somewhat embarrassed to say that during that time I would often read book jacket bios of women authors for clues as to whether to go forward with the family idea. Each time I read "The author lives in New York City with her husband and two children," the scale tipped toward motherhood.

Living in Utah the first two years of Natalie's life, I effortlessly rebelled against the state's Woman as Selfless Mommy paradigm and breast-fed in my college office in between classes. I thought by moving to Seattle I'd be drinking once again from the feminist communal cup, nodding and agreeing with the hipster mothers in Grunge City that as much as we love our children, that's how much we love our own lives as well. But my arrival in Seattle landed me in a preschool coop community that rivaled the Amish in the women's pledge to a certain homespun brand of domesticity. Babies strapped to their chests, the women cooed over their two-year-olds and exchanged techniques for grinding up apples and squash. When questioned (and I did question), these women all seemed to have had tremendous careers in commerce, law, and the like, which they'd given up instantly and without visible struggle for the sake of their children. For a while I wondered if it was just that the women were older than me, which had perhaps made the transition out of career a bit easier, but nope, they were my age: mid-thirties. Yep, mid-thirties and rocking Birkenstocks and dowdy, oversized sweaters. I'd felt better about myself as a mother in Utah, where I was seen as that crazy outsider and could pretend to myself that in my own world I wouldn't be a misfit. But now I *was* in my own world and yet still didn't quite fit in.

As long as I was ensconced in the MFA program, I was pretty okay, my identity bolstered by the camaraderie of my fellow writers, a group of nine of us who spent many an hour in excited discussions about writing. But once the program ended, and I was shuttered into a domestic routine with my very young children, a new, shakier social identity was forged around the other mothers in my daughters' preschool. And it was around then, when I was spending most of my time wiping counters and snapping small people into car seats, that I began to realize how badly suited to full-time motherhood I was and how there was a good chance that this had everything to do with my own childhood.

As I sunk deeper into the lives of my daughters, my childhood started coming back to me in chunks, and I began to see that I'd never had *interested* motherhood modeled to me. My mom, an anomaly in our California neighborhood in the mid-sixties, drove a convertible and owned an insulation contracting business. Glamorous and unapologetically disinterested in all things domestic, my mom found happiness rather readily in a smoky bar talking stocks with a George Clooney look-alike. Part of the unspoken contract between us was that I'd maintain that I was totally good with this, that I even maybe *preferred* a mother on-the-go over a mother in-the-home. But now that it was my turn to give up a portion of adult pursuits and ambition for the welfare of the family—something I was convinced I needed to do in order to be the thing I wanted most to be, a "good mother"—resentment that this same sacrifice had not been made for me began to go from simmer to boil.

Motherhood began to seep into my writing; the crazy overwhelmed feeling that I felt a dozen times a day—I tried to figure it out on the page. But I was afraid of writing about motherhood with too much vigor, lest I find out that I really shouldn't be married to the person to whom I was married, that I was a bad mother, and that I was very angry with my own mother. It was a lot of work to keep all that from myself *and* write *and* teach a few hours a week *and* take care of two kids, but I did it, although not always well. But under the cloak of fiction, I did manage to wrest a story from myself that captured at least a gimlet glass of the truth about my frustration, which became the first piece I ever got published. A short story about a mother of two young children (a boy and a girl, so clearly not me, right?), the story's plot centered around the fluke shooting of the narrator's husband. No anger there! Bonus: The narrator's widowhood status—unlike my own married status—gave her every reason for feeling alone and overwhelmed and alienated from the other mothers in her community.

What does this have to do with finding my own voice? With your finding *your* own voice? Everything. Because it isn't Bach string quartets and split-shot nonfat lattes and generally placid conditions that bring us to our own voices. That's what we *think* will get us there. That's what we *want* to get us there. If I just keep showing up at Starbucks with my laptop, it'll show up, too, right? Maybe. I hope so. But for me it was more like running through fire, feeling like you're going to totally lose it, then trying to act like it's a regular day when you show up at Starbucks with your laptop. And that's pretty much what happened the day that I felt like my real voice was starting to show up on the page. I didn't get there with the two advanced degrees in English (I'm not bragging; in fact, I'm embarrassed that education didn't get me there, to that "real writing place"). I didn't finally get there because I wanted it. I got there because I was desperate.

On this desperate day, I had somehow gotten a one-and-a-half-year-old and a five-year-old dressed and fed and out the door and into the car. All that seems easy, but anyone who's had to do it knows it's not. The rest of you, just picture a really bad day. Now, every day for many days in a row is pretty much like that, and then once in a while a day is really easy—laughing at the park with the kids and effortlessly making dinner—and on that good day you question your sanity. Why are the other days *so hard*?

With my two amazing, beautiful daughters tucked into preschool for the next 1.75 hours, I arrived with my laptop and notepad at the café across from the preschool. It was a nice day and I was sitting outside. Green Lake stretched below me and the Cascades drew a jagged line on the horizon. It was the type of day when one should be thinking: I've got it made. Here I am balancing motherhood and my own interests. I live in a great city! It's sunny!

Instead, I brought out my notepad and let out a low, long growl. My thoughts were something like: Fuck everything, what's the use, grrr, #@!%. I then took out a pen and I wrote this sentence: The women in my family don't really like children.

I looked up. I looked to the preschool and then the lake, waiting for the bolt of lightning to strike me dead. When it did not, I wrote for the next hour and a half about the women in my family. I wrote about being neglected, about being uncared for as a child, I wrote about my mother's distraction and distractions. I wrote about how true nurturing was never modeled to me. How motherhood always seemed to be the last thing on everyone's agenda in my family. And when I wrote "in my family," I meant one thing: my mother.

I know you might be really worried about my mom's feelings right now. I was worried about them, too, but beginning that day and over the next few years I became certain that I had to write about my relationship with my mom—so certain that I might even cart out the word "destiny," as in: I felt it was my *destiny* to write about my relationship with my mother. It's not easy to be a mother whose daughter has taken to writing about you (and there's a good chance that I will have a shot at that experience myself one day, as both my daughters seem to be jotting things down). But it's also not easy to be a daughter who's been holding her mother's denial in her hands for as long as she can remember. It's not easy to be a daughter who was raised to be good in a time when "good" meant quiet. I knew that day—and I still know—that there are a lot of daughters just like me out there, daughters who needed to articulate the inchoate frustration that we've carried in silence for far too long.

I didn't do it for them, though. I did it for me. I did it to survive. And that desperation to survive daughterhood and motherhood brought me to my knees, and it was on my knees that I finally heard it: the unmistakable sound of my own voice coming from the page. And it was saying: Fuck it!

That day I wrote the bones of a piece called "Women Like That, Like Us," an essay born out of the triptych form about my family's tradition of ambivalent (at best) motherhood and how that tradition was showing up on a daily basis in yours truly— about how I wasn't exempt no matter how much I wanted to be. The essay was eventually published in *Brain, Child* magazine and nominated for a prize that meant a lot to me. But the most important thing—in a way, the only important thing—is that it was the first piece of writing I finished that I felt was truly a manifestation of my voice and vision as a writer. I was doing it. I was finally freaking doing it. Thirty-seven years old. Nearly twenty years after I started writing.

And now everyone in the world loves me and is proud of what I do.

No.

And now some people think it's okay and some have been very hurt and angry. A few people really like it.

Yes.

I explain it to my students like this: You know you're near what I call your "real material" when you feel equal parts compulsion to express and terror of expression. It's not enough just to be afraid to tell the story. There are lots of things I'm afraid to write about and which I have no real interest or compulsion to write about. Besides the fear, there also needs to be magnetic pull. Attraction plus terror.

Being a mother and a daughter brought me to my voice, and those roles have complicated everything about my way there. I'd already been a daughter for decades, a role that had for so many years rendered me mute. Not wanting to hurt or offend, I'd kept my real material out of my own reach, up in the highest cupboard. Now it occurred to me that when I'd been fearfully deciding about whether or not to sign up for motherhood, my focus had always been on how motherhood would tie up my time and energy, but in fact there was much more than that at stake. Like the role of daughter, I realized now, the role of mother could also tie up my tongue.

Maybe it was the sleep deprivation or the flawed marriage or I don't know what, but somehow I felt all this crunching down on me. I felt the lifelong boulder of my family's history of alcoholism double in weight with the curiously similar task of keeping silent for the sake of the children.

I was realizing that motherhood meant keeping the peace, keeping things nice and good, keeping the focus on the children. "If you can't say anything nice, don't say anything at all" was back and rearing its head in the hushed banalities exchanged between mothers on the playground. I wanted to have a real conversation about motherhood and couldn't find one—blogs were still a thing of the future—so I started writing what I wanted to hear: how motherhood can break you in two and then slowly build up a new version of yourself, casting aside some of the old parts forever.

Kathryn Harrison was already a mother when she wrote *The Kiss*, a surreal and stunningly beautiful memoir that depicts the incestuous relationship between her and her father when she was a late teen. Among the slew of harsh criticism she received upon the book's publication, some reviewers took issue with the fact that she would write about such things as a mother, the implication clear that part of a mother's job is to shield her children from ugliness—even if it was ugliness she herself had lived through, even if it was an ugliness that had been perpetrated against her. In an interview with *Creative Nonfiction* magazine, Harrison justified her choice as a writer and a mother, saying, in essence, that if she hadn't come forward about her experience with her father, her kids would have sensed something "cordoned off" within their mother and, being kids, might've blamed themselves. I have to say I think she's dead right: Whatever it is we think we're hiding, our children will be asked to carry. But a subtler point here is that mothers who write are often expected to justify their choices of topics and their approach to them, and for some reason we accept this expectation, and I believe this acceptance creates a self-censorship so integral to who we are that its existence often goes undetected.

We have things to do in this life that have nothing to do with the people we love and our relationships with them. We generally accept this for men. For good and for ill, women often have a harder time not focusing on how their actions could potentially impact those around them. If I write what I really feel, the thinking goes, then I will hurt the people I love. And so, sometimes we write nothing at all. Maybe for some that's perfectly okay, but for others it isn't. For many of us there's a sort of festering in the spot where we carry the untold story. We feel tied up in knots. We can talk for an hour about how we wish we had more time. If only I didn't have so much to *do*. If anyone were to suggest that maybe we could do less, we might bite her head off, so invested are we in the sense that all that we do—much of it for other people—is crucial to the continuation of life on the planet. Life as we know it would surely cease if we were to stop the endless activity and sit down with our own thoughts and a pad of paper.

But maybe the end of life as we know it wouldn't be such a bad thing.

Maybe life as we know it keeps those we love dependent on us.

Maybe if we pulled back a bit, they'd step up. And maybe we'd be happier. Less—shall I say it?—resentful?

It's true that my mother often did what she wanted without too much fretting over the consequences for others. It is also true that I have often wished that she were different. When I was a kid, I wanted her to be like the other mothers. When I was a new mother, I wanted her to be like the other grandmothers. But for all that my mother's pursuit of her own pleasure cost me, that's the exact amount I've gained. She loved who she wanted to love. She went where she wanted to go. She drank martinis dry and enjoyed many a steak on the rare side of medium. She took a failing business and single-handedly made it prosper. And on top of that, she did all this in the early 1960s, in the construction industry, as a woman whose education had ended in the tenth grade. She hired and fired men in a man's world. She studied the business pages with the laser intensity of a savant. She bought low, sold high, bought low and sold high—rinse and repeat—until she'd secured the sort of nest egg single mothers of any background or any generation would be hard pressed to replicate.

But her legacy to me isn't so much her success with finance as it is her passion for it. She loved the business world. It consumed her—and she saw no problem with that. Sometimes I hear women talking about how their mothers' martyrdom was a palpable energy in their homes: the sighing, the slammed door, the constant low-level hostility that self-sacrifice often engenders. There were times when I would have liked a bit of self-sacrifice, believe me, but lately—why do we come to it so late?—I realize that my mother modeled a way for me to be a person, a woman, *and* a mother, and that I never could've become the mother who could love her work as she loves her children (yes, *as*) without her example; that without her—whom I'd once believed to be the source of my silence—I never could have found my voice.

If the mother curbs herself for the sake of her family, she becomes less than she can be in the world. And then, what will her daughters do when they have daughters of their own? Will they put themselves on hold endlessly as well? Langston Hughes's enduring question chills me: "What happens to a dream deferred? Does it dry up like a raisin in the sun?"

When I begin with a new group of memoir writing students each year, we go around the room and they introduce themselves and talk about what they'd like to write about. Inevitably, at least one older woman will say, "I want to write stuff down for my grandchildren," which makes my heart sink.

I know that sounds bad. Isn't that what grandmothers do? If that's what she wants to do, why am I judging her? My thinking goes like this: If you're writing stories for your grandchildren, you're going to leave out the time you cheated on a test and lied to your boss, the hot experimental sex you had with your college roommate, how bored you sometimes felt in domestic life, the time you got too drunk at a wedding, the infidelity you considered but then veered away from. These omissions are for good reason. After all, these readers are your *grandchildren*. However, when you take all the crack out of the Cracker Jack, what you're left with is . . . not much. You're left with the literary equivalent of one of the more tepid episodes of *The Waltons*: a highly sanitized version of your life.

More bad news: Ninety percent of the time, your grandchildren won't read what you wrote—even if you had put all that juicy stuff in there, which you didn't. They know the juicy stuff isn't in there. They actually don't think you even own any juicy stuff because you're their grandmother, and they still believe that the young have the juice market cornered. They will thank you when they receive the bound edition of *Grandma's Life* on Christmas morning, maybe even skimming a page right there in front of you, but then they'll put it aside, always meaning to get to it but never quite. Recently, one of my students had some of her work published for the first time in a literary journal and sent copies to family members. "Theo, I never heard anything back," she said to me, surprised and disappointed. "Do you think they hate what I wrote?"

"No. They haven't read it," I said, adding: "People don't read."

Okay, that last part isn't quite true. People *do* read, but they don't necessarily read what we want them to read, even when they are our own family and even when we are handing them our own writing. *Especially* our own writing when we hand it to them.

So let's go back to this book you wrote for your grandchildren, the book you spent hours creating—hundreds and hundreds of hours, I exaggerate not; the book you created with a specific audience in mind; the book that's only a shadow of what it could be because it was created *for family*; a document that was alternately pleasant and onerous to write, but was never liberating, never truly intoxicating. It was a story eternally fettered to the ground like a falcon in a zoo exhibit.

But what if it could have flown?

What if you *had* written it for yourself?

What if after all those Thanksgiving turkeys and elaborate Christmas mornings you put your efforts into something *for yourself* with no communal gain in mind? If your family ends up reading it and even liking it, all the better, but what if you started out on this adventure with only your own literary vision and your own fulfillment in mind? The tribe might profit from your work in the end—who knows?—but that would be an accidental by-product of this writing, not its raison d'être.

No. Its reason for being—your reason for picking up the pen and showing up at the page—would be this: You want it. You *want* it. You want the paper under your hand, smooth and gliding like a bedsheet. You crave the pen in your hand, carving out the meaning only you can create.

You are not bad, or selfish, for wanting this for yourself. In fact, your writing's one shot of coming into its own—of truly offering something fabulous to the world—depends upon the existence of this type of animal selfishness. For in the deep desire to express what is truly our own, we have that one golden opportunity to tell that which belongs to all of us: the universal story of love and loss, of despair and redemption, of our trespasses and our forgiveness.

We give most to others when we are fully ourselves. "Don't ask what the world needs," philosopher Howard Thurman once said. "Ask what makes you come alive, and go do it. Because what the world needs is people who have come alive."

So go on, pick up the pen. Come alive.

TRY THIS

1. Write on this question: How have you kept silent or limited your writing because you feel that somehow you owe this silence or limited articulation to another family member?

2. Has that same family member ever actually been the impetus in some way for your writing? How can you credit them for their contribution to your eagerness to write?

3. Write on this question: What writers do you really admire? And what can you specifically point to in their work that you can imagine some family member somewhere is not too happy about? How different or less powerful would that writing be without those elements? What would be lost?

4. Write on this question: How have those writings helped you? How have you benefited from other writers' willingness to tell family secrets, to call out issues, to speak the unspeakable? For many of us, the only place we've ever been able to see our own experience reflected back to us is in books. As James Baldwin said, "You think your pain and your heartbreak are unprecedented in the history of the world, but then you read. It was books that taught me that the things that tormented me most were the very things that connected me with all the people who were alive, or who had ever been alive."

5. If you are a mother, write on this topic: How has being a mother inhibited you as a writer? And how has being a mother fueled you as a writer?

6. Have you limited your own writing to protect your own

mother? And yes, even after they die, sometimes we still remain very busy protecting our mothers.

7. Answer this question as quickly as you can: What do you want to write for yourself? What is your vision of that project? What's the tone of it? What does it feel like to you?

11

A Couple of Irishmen
Walk into a Bar

The first thing I noticed about Frank McCourt was his voice, or rather my dad's voice coming from his mouth. I guess it makes sense that they would have similar accents: Born within a few years of each other to Irish parents, both Bill and Frank spent part of their childhoods in Ireland and part in the New World. It all made perfect sense, but the logic didn't muffle the impact or negate the sense I had that for a week of the summer of 2003, Frank McCourt became the pinch hitter filling in the dad-sized hole in my heart.

The location for my Frank encounter was the Southampton Writers Conference. For this one July week, I slept in a cinderblock dorm room by night and sat at a desk in Frank's memoir workshop by day, there in the Hamptons, perched on a tiny campus flanked by mansions just a few miles from the fabled beaches.

Truth be told, I'd arrived at the feet of the master not much in the mood for learning. I'm not proud of this, as I'm not proud of other times when I've been too self-absorbed to notice meteors streaking across the sky or yawned in the face of a perfect sunset. But being ashamed doesn't change the fact that I was restless and irritable from waiting, waiting, and waiting to hear if my agent thought my manuscript was ready to send out. The book was a memoir about motherhood called *Light Sleeper: The Making of an Unlikely Mother*. Getting to this point had been a long uphill push—writing the manuscript, finding the agent, and then revising the manuscript based on her recommendations.

Besides my impatience with my dragging-feet agent, other problems clamored for my attention too. Every time I called home, something seemed irreparably off with my husband and me. An ominous cloud hung over every conversation. I'd hang up knowing there was a problem, and then call back and say something like "Is it just me or was that weird?" and then it would get worse. Then I'd hang up and lie on the bed with the sinking heart that knows something is wrong, even if that something cannot be named. I felt insanely far from home. I wanted desperately to go back and make it all better, but I also knew that going home, which would inevitably come at the end of the week anyway, would do no good at all. In the midst of all this, a group of us writers went to a local Long Island dive bar one night, and an older poet grabbed me out of the blue (really, no flirting, nothing) and kissed me long and hard like an errant messenger sent with a partial answer to that What's-wrong? question that had been dogging me.

This was the agitated state of mind I brought to Frank's memoir class. I had a strong sense that I was a person waiting to be blasted from one location to the next. In my delusional state, I thought that rocket boost might be about to take me from obscurity to literary glory, though the truth was I was about to be blasted from marriage to divorce.

Frank's class, I realized very quickly, was no place for the mentally restless. An accomplished and languid storyteller, Frank could easily take an hour of class time to tell a story or five. As he told us about his life as a teacher in the New York City public school system, a divorce, family entanglements, and what some priest back in Ireland thought of *'Tis*, I anxiously waited for class to start, for him to tell me what I needed to do to become published in a big way.

At some point, I think during class two, I realized: This really was *it*. Frank was a storyteller. *Angela's Ashes* was the stellar success that it was because Frank knows something—everything—about how to tell a story. Sometime during that class, as Frank taught us everything he knew about setting, dialogue, pacing, and theme by laying his stories down before us one by one, my resistance wore down. I regressed further and further back in time until at last I landed back at the dining room table where my dad had routinely held court for hours. Plate pushed aside, a pack of Peter Jacksons in front of him, my dad could tell an endless story, pausing only for emphasis and to take a long draw off his gin and tonic. Like Frank, my dad's Irish accent was diluted by North America, a tendency toward the emphatic rather than a true brogue. And now, listening by the hour to Frank, I was back home with my dad once again.

Our home—the patched-together family home that my mother and stepfather created together—often had the atmosphere of a pub. Stray work associates regularly congregated in the living room during cocktail hour for a couple rounds of 7&7s or gin and tonics or Molson Old Style served in frosty steins. Out would come an array of savory snacks, perfect for the adult drinker's numbed palate: pickled eggs and herring, peppery crackers, smoked almonds, sardines dripping with oil. A blue cloud formed under the ceiling as the ashtrays filled. In our basement was a player piano around which a handful of forty-somethings would cluster late in the evening, singing along to "The Caissons Go Rolling Along" and "You Must Have Been a Beautiful Baby" as my dad pumped the pedals, a smoke hanging from his lower lip. These were the good times: These moments of frolicking entertaining were what my parents were destined to create together, and when they were living out their twinned fate, I felt free to live out my own.

My dad had a magnetic personality, a restless curiosity, and a laser focus for the cares and concerns of others; people flocked to him for his stories and for his counsel. I, too, loved listening to him, but when there was no party, I felt like my role of conversation partner/listener went from optional to mandatory. My parents couldn't exist alone together; they needed the oxygen an audience can provide. When I was in the twelfth grade, the jubilant pub nights faded away when two things happened that abruptly changed the course and tenor of my family's life: The first was when my dad was transferred from his downtown executive position to a mill manager's position in a damp mill town on Vancouver Island.

Outrageous independence was the expected norm for youth both in the single-mom family I'd known in California and in the pub night family of my teens. It was, partly, the times. When I tell family tales from the sixties and seventies, people sometimes nod and say glibly, "That's how it was back then." But my family took this laissez-faire parenting to an extreme. For example, shortly after my mom and Bill married in a California ceremony without any of their children present, I flew alone at age ten to my new home in Canada. While our newly wedded parents slowly honeymooned their way up the Pacific Coast Highway, I was fetched from immigration at the Vancouver airport by my sullen, newly minted teenage stepsiblings, who were solely responsible for my care during my first week in my new home in a new country. Not exactly *Leave It to Beaver* material.

And our move during my senior year to Nanaimo, once known as the heroin capital of Canada, was not much different. For some reason, my parents weren't ready to make the move themselves in time for my first day of school. So I ferried over alone from Horseshoe Bay to Vancouver Island with my dad's late-model Renault and spent the night before the first day at my new high school alone in the Port-O-Call motel on Terminal Avenue. My mom told me this would be "exciting." I found it "terrifying." However, because I was told it would be "exciting," I couldn't register my terror fully, only noting a peculiar numb sensation in my limbs as I pointed the Renault north toward Nanaimo District Senior Secondary. My new school was the gathering point for every working-class teen within a forty-mile radius of wet fir trees surrounding the epicenter known as Harmac, the union mill where my father would soon become one of the loathed group known as *management*.

Overnight, our home had gone from urbane social hub

to pioneer outpost. Once in a while my mom would drag in a neighbor woman for a glass of Chablis or my dad would bring home one of the other managers from the mill, but for the most part we were on our own. All of my friends were back in the city, and I was floundering around the halls of my new school with no clue how to make friends with kids who drove Ford F-150s and listened to Black Sabbath. The three of us were stuck with one another.

But it was more than the move that turned the lights out on the party and moved my role of listener up to front and center. Much more. Just before my dad's job change, my twenty-three-year-old stepsister, Barbara, who was living in Vancouver attending her last year at university, started to get sick. She couldn't eat and began to lose a lot of weight, and then tests confirmed the worst: It was cancer. It's strange how the mind can remember so many details and yet be unsure about a crucial sequence of events, but I'm fairly sure that it was in our first few months in our new mill town life that we realized that Barbara's cancer was terminal.

As hope for her recovery faded, the light within my dad—his seemingly endless energy and optimism—began to go out. His withdrawal from life was palpable. I felt desperate to hang on to him, to keep alive some semblance of the happier times, but I was also preoccupied with problems of my own. For the first time ever, I could say without exaggeration that I hated my life. I despised my new school and couldn't see any hope of the situation improving. My mom's suggestions of "conversation starters" and joining clubs were absurd. As the city slicker, I had as much chance of cracking this social scene as I had of getting invited to Buckingham Palace for tea. I missed my old life, Kansas and Auntie Em, and all I could think of was how to get back, which is what I did several hours a day in my dark basement bedroom, listening to the rain thrashing against the windows and *The Best of Bread* on auto repeat.

The social buoyancy of our city life had held us together, and here in our new isolation we seemed less like a family and more like three desperate strangers on a train to nowhere. Barbara's illness also exposed the fissures in our blended family. It was my dad's daughter who was dying, not my mother's. My dad was howlingly sad without the ability to howl. My mom wasn't *as sad*. It wasn't that she wasn't sad: She was sad in the way one is sad when losing a stepchild one does not get along with particularly well. My dad's was the wrenching grief of a parent losing a child. The dark subtext below the disparity between their emotional states was something that no one—no matter how much or how little they'd had to drink—ever mentioned: the fact that Barbara and my mother had never liked each other very much. No *Brady Bunch* episode had covered this one.

While my sister's dying was my loss as well, it was silently understood to be a mitigated loss; after all she wasn't really my sister, and she'd only been my stepsister for seven years. In the hierarchy of loss, mine barely registered, which made me ostensibly available to fill the role that under other circumstances would've been my mother's: the role of listener. Being the listener meant being the receiver of stories, of wisdom, of insights. Sitting in the listener's seat meant attending to another person's need to tell a story, which for me meant putting on hold my own need to express. I was never *asked* to just listen, but I felt with my new dad, my grieving dad, that listen was all I could do.

Back in the role of listener in Frank's class—after the lion of my ambition temporarily gave up the hunt and found a shady spot in the corner to collapse—I fell drowsily under the spell of Frank's dad voice. His stories were intimate, and like the other students in the class I quickly felt as if I knew Frank better than I actually did. Within the first days I had the sense that Frank was someone I'd known most of my life. His stories were full of longing: a longing to write, for recognition, for home. His voice was a minor chord in an Irish key—the perfect pitch for the stories of what might have been and for making me long to have my dad back: not just my dad as I knew him before he died in 1997 but my dad as I knew him in a time when all things were still possible; my dad of pub nights; my dad before he knew his daughter was dying, before innocence was lost. I still needed my dad and yet he was gone. But Frank—my one-week father *in loco*, arguably the father of the modern memoir—was here, and that comforted me.

In the role of listener, I found myself thinking about the role of the storyteller and what it takes to earn your audience's consent to hold the floor. Recently, one of my students told me that's why she wants to publish her memoir. "It's like you're at a party and everyone is taking their turn to talk. I feel like 'Okay, it's my turn to tell my story.'" The need for a turn is a primary one. And as I listened, I realized the most obvious thing in the world: The storyteller is the person sitting in the power seat, the seat that I'd secretly and not so secretly yearned for since my dining room table days. Of course, Frank had an extra boost of power because he was a Pulitzer Prize winner, a *New York Times* best-selling author, and one of the few living authors who was nearly a household name. But maybe it was the reverse; maybe he became a celebrated writer because he was powerful, because knowing how to hold the floor was his gift.

When I met my stepfather Bill, I was functionally fatherless, living in an extended family of women without a male in sight in the days before feminism was back on the map. I was a kid who'd lived outside of the power circle all my life, and it seemed like I absorbed the impact of all Bill's starched-white-shirt power in an instant. Everything that I learned about him after that simply supported my initial assumption of his regency: the casual way he held the menu as he ordered for the whole table; the way his beige trench coat folded perfectly over his arm; the way he entered a room, a conversation, or a relationship as if he had the right to be there, and that there was nowhere in the world where he'd be excluded or unwanted; the way he argued about world affairs as if they were matters of personal business—as if his opinions might change the course of nations, even when the setting for that oration was just a dining room table and his only audience a teenage girl.

Bill spoke French, had studied engineering at McGill, worked in downtown Vancouver at the top of a very tall building, and occasionally was interviewed for the nightly news. He knew manners I had never imagined existed: working your way through the silverware from the outside in, the role of the butter knife and its relationship to the very important bread plate, the napkin unfolded halfway on your lap, the importance of the question "Whom may I say is calling?" He told me that proper manners would ensure that I'd be comfortable dining with "presidents, queens, or ordinary people," which invited me to imagine a tremendous future unfurling in front of me like a red carpet, a future full of dignitaries and foreign travel. He treated everyone with respect, a behavior I understood to be a function of his power; he could afford to be respectful because he himself was treated with respect.

Of all these displays of privilege and power, however, none seemed as remarkable as his ability to hold the floor. The circumstances didn't seem to matter; when he spoke, people fell quiet and listened. I loved the sound not only of his voice but also of the silence around his voice. The hush. What could be more powerful than people listening to what you say? For most of my adolescence, it didn't occur to me that power could be mine. Wasn't it enough to warm my hands by its fire?

I had that same feeling as I watched the class fall under Frank's spell as he acted out conversations with truculent, inner-city youth and described scenes sitting by the fire, writing *Angela's Ashes* in longhand, the tenor of his story rising into crescendos and then falling back almost to a hushed whisper. When my stepfather died, it felt like I'd lost my connection to this brand of power. But those days in Frank's classroom made me feel like it was within reach again, that maybe he could hand it to me.

• • •

On the second night of the conference, a book signing and cocktail party was held in one of the main campus buildings. Because of its Hamptons location, the conference skewed a little less literary and a tad more *People* magazine than most writers' conferences. Lesser-known celebrities nipped in and out, attending random readings and lunches. I spent a good bit of mental energy trying to figure out how this odd assortment of people were connected to each other and never truly cracked the code, but amongst us commoners a familiar face would occasionally drift—Jane Pauley, Garry Trudeau, Alan Alda—and not wanting to be total buffoons, most of us fledgling writers pretended it was natural to be standing in the bathroom line with Jane Pauley. Oh, but of course, Mel Brooks has dropped by.

The social incongruence of these odd celebrity sightings in a social setting more commonly known for its dowdiness added to my feeling of displacement in the world. A West Coaster in the Hamptons, a married woman whose marriage was about to blow apart, I walked into the book party with my social anxiety dialed to high until I spotted Frank across the room.

I made my way over to him and asked him to sign my copy of *Angela's Ashes*, which he did, and I put the book into my purse. Then the flock of fans around him grew, and I drifted away and found wine, food, and other fledgling writers to hang out with. That night back in my dorm room, I finally dug my *Angela's Ashes* out of my purse. I turned to the title page, and there it was in his scrawl: "For Theo—To a hell of a writer! Frank McCourt." I closed the book and opened it again. It was still there: the casual endorsement that made me feel like I'd been handed a bolt of lightning. And that loose but old-fashioned cursive: It could've been my dad's.

After my parents married in a private ceremony at the retirement center where my grandmother, Nonnie, lived, my new dad, my mom, and I went to Los Angeles to stay with a friend of my mom's for a few days. I'd just turned ten, so it didn't occur to me to question the sanity of two middle-age people marrying each other after just one year of long-distance dating, to question the fact that my new brother and sister had met me just one time.

In the course of the next year, my mother, Bill, and I silently colluded in the process of erasing whatever wisp of a tie I might still have had with my real father. Shouting out from a Topanga Canyon swimming pool, I called Bill "Dad" for the first time. I had to get up my nerve to do it, like I was asking for a raise. I thought maybe calling it from my spot at the lip of the pool to his chaise lounge was a safe experiment. When he turned automatically without a flinch, I decided that was it: He would be "Dad" from there on out. I wouldn't turn back. It had taken too much for me to take that first step toward him, ground too hard earned to ever surrender.

My dad began teaching me everything I imagine girls with fathers know. The first job he took on was teaching me to dive, a daunting task if there ever was one. His hours of patient coaching resulted in a total of one completed dive, results that encouraged him enough to go on to teach one of the most physically timid children in the history of civilization to water-ski, to snow ski, and, later, to drive stick. When we arrived in Canada, my mother registered me in school under my stepfather's name. No birth certificate was needed back then to support her claim. From then on, I was my dad's girl, an Irish girl without a drop of Irish blood, a Mehaffey. But I would always understand myself to be an impostor, a girl who was passing as connected, as fathered, as more powerful than she actually was.

That week in the Hamptons, when I wasn't in Frank's class, I was using my time productively: alternating between disheartening calls home and obsessive e-mail checking as I waited to hear some news from my agent. Finally, there was an e-mail from the agent's assistant, who suggested it wouldn't be a bad idea to ask Frank for a letter of support. It could help, she said. A lot.

Ask?

Sure, and then I'll dive into icy, shark-infested water and take a swim. Ask? Even the word, when isolated from other words, sounds frightening: "Ask."

I walked away from the computer and stumbled across the manicured lawns toward my cinder-block dorm room. Ask. How insane was that? Who would do that?

Throughout the week Frank held one-on-one meetings with each of his students. It's a generous thing to do—anyone who's taught will tell you that. It always takes more time and energy than the half-hour allotted meeting time would suggest. My meeting was on Thursday, and by Wednesday afternoon I was convinced that I needed to ask him for the letter. It was a risk worth taking. I knew it bordered on outrageous, since he barely knew me well enough to write such a letter, but I also knew that publishing was full of endorsements built on more tenuous connections and that endorsements made a difference. But all that didn't stop me from being crazy scared. Besides fear of rejection, I worried that whatever small impression I'd made on him might change. I wanted for him to know that I genuinely liked him and appreciated him. I didn't want him to see me as yet another person who wanted something from him, although of course that's exactly what I was.

I'm a one-on-one person. I get a little confused in groups, a social vertigo that perhaps is the result of having been raised as if I were an only child. In groups, I don't know which way is up or where to look and what's okay to say and what's not. I either say barely anything at all or hog the floor with frantic ramblings and show tunes. When I like someone, I want them to myself, and when I have one-on-one time with someone I like or admire, I am disproportionately jubilant. And so as anxious as I was about my individual meeting with Frank McCourt, part of me was giddy with the idea of getting to talk to Frank all by myself. And so during our meeting I had this odd sensation of bifurcation: Part of me was sitting in the classroom, the other was up on the ceiling pointing down and saying, "Look! There she is, talking with Frank McCourt about writing!"

Down on the ground, Frank and I talked about my *Light Sleeper* manuscript, which for some reason I'd dragged into the meeting with me. I told him about the slow-footed agent, and he listened sympathetically and then pointed to the manuscript beside me and asked, "So, is it honest?"

Uh. *Light Sleeper*—I can trash it a bit because (1) I wrote it and (2) I know now that it's never going to be published—was not a terrible book and not a dishonest book. In fact, it was pretty honest about my own aversion to parenting and my slow conversion to involved motherhood. Yet, I knew even then that there was something missing, though I didn't understand then that the problem lay in the narrator's complete glossing over of her marriage. A few months after this meeting with Frank, the marital fissure the memoir had nicely plastered over would become impossible to ignore, but I wasn't there yet.

I looked at Frank. Like my dad, Frank had sad eyes in a happy face. Like my dad, he expected you to tell him the truth.

"It seems like there's levels of honesty, right?" I finally said.

"Go on," he said, leaning forward.

"Well," I said, stalling a bit, as I really didn't know what I was about to say. "You can write a memoir that goes this deep"—I waved my flattened hand to indicate the level of the desktop—"and people will say, that's honest, that's brave, maybe even 'Wow.'"

"But?" Frank said, leading me into the water a little further.

"But there's a much deeper story. Maybe it's down here," I said, my hand waving between our knees. "And maybe nobody but you knows it, but if you told *that* story, that would be the really honest one."

"I like that," he said, leaning back in his chair, making me think for a millisecond that I was off the hook. "And so, where's this book?"

I paused just for a beat and then leveled my hand just slightly under the desktop, saying, "Maybe here."

"Not bad," he said, "not bad."

We talked a bit more about other things—about the conference, the weather—and then it was clearly time for me to go. It was the do-or-die moment, and my heart was beating very quickly.

"So, one more thing," I said, meeting his gaze. "Would you be comfortable writing a note of support for my writing?"

He looked a bit shocked but recovered quickly. "I'd be happy to," he said.

I thanked him profusely, and with a great deal of awkwardness I made it out of the chair and out the door.

I received the letter in the mail six weeks later, and what surprised me the most was that it was handwritten. Then I remembered the contempt he'd shown in class for writing done on computers. "It's not writing," he'd said. "It's just tapping."

I read the letter over and over and then I folded it carefully and put it back in the envelope. He told "To Whom It May Concern" that I was a writer who would be heard from. "Yes, she'll be heard from," he repeated at the end, convincing me finally. I understood now that no matter whom I might pass this letter along to, the letter was for me. It was a letter of encouragement. It was the letter from an older person telling a younger person that they can do it. Sometimes those older people are fathers. Sometimes they're fathers telling you that they are proud of you.

. . .

There's a fine line between sitting on a barstool telling stories and writing a memoir. Part of my inheritance as a writer is a feeling of being off-center, of being a transplant, an impostor; but another part of it is the New World Irish culture in which I came of age, a culture where sitting around, swapping endless stories, is a completely legit way to spend a Friday night; a world where the person who knows exactly how long to pause after the phrase "and then I said to him" is the person who holds the floor the longest.

When I went to register for college, the registrar pointed out the disconnect between the last name on my birth certificate (my biological father's) and that on my high school transcripts (my stepdad's). I no longer wanted to feel like an impostor, so I changed my last name back to "Nestor," but I still felt like an impostor and I still felt like I belonged to my stepfather.

When I finally got the chance to use the blurb Frank had written, it wasn't for the motherhood manuscript that had sat between us that day. It was for a memoir about my divorce. I worried that I was stealing the words from him, that I was once again an impostor, but when my editor tracked him down to make sure he was okay with me using the quote, he wrote back, "You can quote me from here to infinity."

Frank, I will.

TRY THIS

1. Think about two people in your life who've taught you a similar lesson. Write about those two people in one story united by the lesson's theme.

2. Think about a recent piece you've written or a piece you are currently writing and answer Frank's question: "Is it honest?" If the answer is no, write for ten minutes on the topic of the piece more honestly, reassuring yourself that no one needs to see what you've written. You can decide later what you want to do with this new honesty, but for now just let yourself go to that deeper level.

3. A literary legacy can be as simple as having a family tradition of storytelling. Identify your literary legacy. Write for ten minutes on these questions: What did you learn about storytelling in your family? Who were the people who held the floor? What did you learn from them?

4. Write about this question: What did you learn from your father about storytelling or about having a voice and power in the world? How was it similar to or different from what you learned from your mother?

12

F is for "Failure," "Flawed," and "All Effed-up"

There is no way to become a published writer without becoming a rejected writer. There is no way to succeed—whatever your vision of success might be—without going through a dark tunnel of failure, though how long that tunnel will be for you, I cannot say. And even when you've achieved whatever benchmark you've labeled for yourself as "success"—maybe somewhere between your mom's friends at her retirement center thinking you're great and jetting to Sweden to pick up your Nobel Prize—you will still continue to be rejected. You will still fail. You might as well get used to it. A wise therapist once said to me, "You can't avoid heartbreak, and if you try, you'll just end up living a half a life and you will *still* experience heartbreak."

It seems to me that living a half a life is in *itself* heartbreaking. Rejection can be painful, but for writers, it is an unavoid-

177

able occupational hazard. Every work has its troubles. This is ours. Don't avoid the sting. Keep writing. Keep sending out your work.

I know: Easier said than done.

Most of us can't help but take rejection personally, can't help but interpret rejection to mean that we're not good enough. Whenever my work is rejected, I am instantly that eight-year-old girl with the lick of hair standing straight up in the class picture, the girl whose paper has ripped from desperate erasing. It doesn't take much for me to flash to the shame place, that hot spot in my core that emits the cellular message that I'm inadequate, that there's a flaw that runs through the stone, that I really am the girl who—as my sixth-grade teacher noted on my report card—makes "deplorable errors."

Sometimes, we don't even need anyone else to turn our work down. We do it ourselves. After a few months or even a few years of writing, we look at our work and all we can see is how far short of the mark it falls compared to, say, Alice Munro's or Chekhov's. But writing has an insanely long apprenticeship period. It's practically un-American to say that you might work at something for a decade before getting results that don't make you cringe, but in my experience and from what I've seen in other writers' careers, that ten-year estimate is not unreasonable. That ten years can be full of minor and major commercial successes and "failures," but no matter how the reading and buying public might be experiencing us, we are not fully cooked as writers for many years. Yes, there are a few boy and girl wonders out there, but they're the exception not the rule. The rule is long hours. The rule is low pay or no pay.

The list of what we can't control is endless. We can't control how others will read our work, who will like it and who will not. We can't control acceptance. I've heard the suggestion: "Do your part and then let go of the results." To say that following this advice has been a struggle for me is an understatement. I've always been obsessed with results. When I first started to send out work after grad school, I wanted publication with a fever akin to lust. I craved it with my entire being. And on the positive side of the equation, that craving—as most cravings do—set off a chain of activity needed to reach my goal: researching magazines, writing, networking, asking questions, more writing, attending readings and conferences, rewriting.

The dark side of the craving was the conviction that this hunger could be satisfied by a single external source and obsessive thinking about how that source might manifest. I was a bit ashamed of my lust for publication. I tried to keep the extent of my desire under wraps. I remember hitting an apex with this frustrated desire in early 2002. I went to a reading by Terry Tempest Williams at Town Hall in Seattle, where she read a beautiful, moving piece about 9/11. It was the first time I'd heard a writer's take on 9/11 and I was moved by her description, but also by her presence and her authenticity. I felt an awe for her stature as a writer and a public person, which had grown considerably since I'd met her six years earlier.

After the reading, I lined up with a zillion other people for a book signing. I was eager to reconnect with her again, although I doubted she'd remember me. But when it was my turn and I said "I don't know if you remember me . . ." she jumped in and said she remembered me from the faculty development seminar in Utah a few years back. She wanted to know what I was doing now—she was very gracious and seemingly interested—and I told her about coming to Seattle to do an MFA and my fledgling writing career. And then it was time to go.

On the drive home, I felt sorrow fill me from my shoulders to my feet. Why should I feel sad? I had a nice evening. I got to talk to Terry, who'd been a role model for me and who I still looked up to as a person of letters who used her gift to make people think and feel. Why shouldn't that make me happy? Was I jealous? That seemed a likely answer, but it wasn't quite it. And then I realized I was sad because I wanted to be a peer or at least a near peer to Terry. I didn't want to be a fledgling writer any longer. I wanted the two of us to share something genuine. I wanted to be in her tribe.

I realized that this was part of why I was so hungry for publication. I wanted to be recognized as a writer and I wanted to be a part of a community of writers as a peer, not as a groupie. It seemed that I had more in common with writers than with any other group of people. Except for one thing: I was barely published. How would my people recognize me until I had proven myself as a writer?

It was dawning on me that my lust for publication wasn't shameful. Yes, I wanted glory, fame, and gold, but mostly I wanted recognition and legitimate membership in the community I already considered my own. And I wanted something else: a readership. I wanted people who were not my friends or blood relatives to read my work. I wanted my work to stir them the way that I had been stirred by Terry both that night and six years earlier when she'd stood in her conservative home state and read from a book that speaks boldly of her complicated relationship with her culture. I wanted to hear the hush around my words. I wanted my words to stir up the molecules in a room.

Was that so bad?

There are certain experiences—like loneliness, grief, and failure—that seem to permeate our lives but for which we seem as a culture to have not enough ways to discuss. Almost everyone I know has been lonely, but no one ever seems to admit it. Grief is a constant in life, and yet no one wants to hear about it for long. We're supposed to get over stuff, to move on. Failure—and feelings of failure—permeate even the most successful of lives, and yet there seem so few ways to make sense of the times we've reached and fallen.

So I was really excited to hear Joyce Carol Oates talk about failure as not only a routine part of a writer's career pattern but even perhaps a desirable one. At a 2011 Seattle Arts & Lectures talk, Oates eloquently argued the point, which she has also made in her essay "Notes on Failure," that early commercial success can actually *stunt* a writer's progress and early "failure" can contribute to a writer's eventual success. Her theory is that if a writer is very successful commercially with an early book, he or she will keep writing that very same type of book, which, in fact, may not be all that good and may actually be highly derivative of an already established author the emerging writer is unconsciously or even consciously imitating. But if an author bombs out with her or his first and second novels, the author may then be given the "opportunity" to forget about the marketplace and just for the hell of it write a second or third book that is truly in his own voice and thus more likely to be of literary value.

Oates cited Faulkner as a perfect example of this: His first three books, she said, were horrible. One book, *Mosquitoes*, was a complete Hemingway knockoff, and the other two were also pale imitations of other fashionable writers of the time. And then, Oates said, his apprenticeship came to an end—just when a writer of less courage might've given up—and he knocked it out of the park with *The Sound and the Fury* (1929) and then *As I Lay Dying* (1930) and then *Sanctuary* (1931). The rest is literary history.

But even if early commercial flops and flat-out publishing rejections might be necessary or even, as Oates argues, *good* for the writer in the long haul, that isn't how it feels when the world tells us there is definitely no room at the inn, that in no uncertain terms our essay, story, or whatever we've created will not be appearing in the next issue of *Fabulous* magazine, when we hear the perennial "No, thanks." Or, in the language of book publishers everywhere: "I was charmed by the author's voice and found the writing very engaging. That said, I'm afraid I'll have to pass on this. Best of luck finding this manuscript a good home!"

"That said."

Puh-lease.

Who says that?

Agents and editors. That's it.

And in the fall of 2003, I hear enough "That saids" to last a lifetime. Three weeks after I received Frank's nice letter, my life began to unravel fast. My husband and I split up the last week of September, just as my agent was about to send out my manuscript depicting a fairly happily married woman's conversion to motherhood. Two weeks after the split, I rewrote the end of *Light Sleeper*, quickly bringing the marriage to a halt in the manuscript's final pages. It took months for all the rejections from round one to roll in and then it went out for another round. "Yes comes fast," someone told me, "and no comes slow or never at all." So true.

By Christmas, I'd almost accepted my defeat, but not quite. I hung on to hope, parsing through the rejection letters to find evidence that the book had enough spark to ignite faith in some editor somewhere. I wanted the publication for all the right reasons (recognition of my work, community membership, an audience) and all the deluded ones (mega money that would solve all my problems, validation that I was a worthy human being, freedom from the bondage of the "loser" title I felt was now mine).

But it wasn't until late spring that I heard that the agent was definitely no longer interested in sending out the book. It was over. The three-year *Light Sleeper* dream was ending, and now I was stunningly awake and surveying the debris of my life. No big advance was on the way. I was a woman with two young kids and a part-time teaching job in the middle of a divorce. My writing wasn't going to save me.

I guess what happened to me next Oates might call a good thing. I developed a big, liberating screw-you attitude. As miserable as I was, there was something remarkable and astonishing at how spectacularly I'd failed in the arenas of both work and home with alarming synchronicity, and yet here I was: still breathing, living, sometimes even laughing, sometimes even laughing demonically. Just a sliver of me felt like a tough chick, like: Yeah, I'm divorced. Yeah, my book crashed. So what? Wanna make something of it, huh? And then, that faux badass part of me began to grow. I smoked a couple of pilfered cigs on the back porch after the kids went to bed and knocked back a cognac. Nothing to lose now.

Intoxicated by defeat, I opened up the file of notes I'd been taking on my divorce and started writing them out into small, unpublishable scenes. I refused to craft them into one continuous story that might make them into something publishable, because I now saw publishing as a closed door. So I would be an *artiste*. Misunderstood, brooding, creating reckless collages, that would be me. When my agent—ahem, former agent—had first seen my *Light Sleeper*, it was a collection of essays. "You can't sell an essay collection unless you're Anna Quindlen," she'd said. "Turn it into one consecutive narrative and then I can sell it." So that's what I had done. I spent months picking out the stitches of the essays and reconstructing it into what was supposed to be a "marketable," seamless narrative with helpful transitions.

Where had all that got me? Nowhere. In hindsight, the truth was the revision had taken the charge out of whatever electricity had once existed in the book. The book might have arguably become more marketable (although that's hard to argue, seeing as it never found a buyer) but it didn't become a better book. And worse, I'd lost that loving feeling I'd once had for writing, and it wasn't just the rejection that had killed my buzz. In unstitching my collage-style essays, I'd lost something. My voice.

Now that I was destined for a life of failure, what did it matter what I wrote? I might as well, I figured, write just for myself. I could still remember my days back in Utah, sitting on the poet's trailer floor or in the lodge surrounded by cedars back when publication was more than unattainable—it was unimaginable. I still remembered what love felt like. Back in those early days, my one wish was just to complete something, to finish a story that felt like it had something of me in it.

Alone in my old, falling-apart house, I turned to my notepad when my kids were in school and wrote scenes from my divorce with one goal in mind: I wanted to capture the stunning feeling of sudden loss and isolation. Articulation felt like the one ticket out of my desperation. If I could create some sort of meaning on the page, I could rebuild hope.

As I wrote, I decided that those pages were only for me. No one else. It was a giant message to myself about my own importance at a time when I felt invisible and of no consequence. Even if I was the only reader of this writing, I was a reader. I counted. For that moment in time, I was the only audience I cared about. Born out of grief, despair, and a sacred place of zero expectations, the words came rapidly. I filled pages much quicker than my usual slow, cautious pace. I was writing with abandon, and I found myself liking what I wrote—liking it, in fact, quite a bit.

Around this time, one of the editors of *Brain, Child* magazine—the mag that had published my very first story—got back in touch with me. She was doing a story about "momoirs" and wanted to interview me about my failed attempt to publish mine. My first instinct was to say no, but then something nudged me forward. Of course, I'd much rather be interviewed about my smashing success, but I'd had very few opportunities lately to interact with the world beyond the grocery store and my kids' school and knew I shouldn't pass one by. Yes, it was humbling, but humble was where I was at.

Not long after that, I got a letter in the mail with some good news. I'd been awarded a scholar spot at that summer's upcoming Bread Loaf Writers' Conference, an honor that I'd always read as a sign of imminent success since I attended the conference for the first time as a participant in 2001. I had nothing else to submit for a workshop piece, so I sent a hunk of the divorce material. I went to the conference and had a great time making new friends, and after the conference my workshop leader sent me an e-mail. A friend of his was starting a column about relationships for the *New York Times* called "Modern Love." He thought my divorce piece would be a good match for the column. Was I interested in submitting?

I read the e-mail thinking, Yeah, that's never going to happen, but went ahead and contacted the editor. I was risking rejection again, this time with the work that I truly considered my own, work in which there was no compromise. There would be no escape hatch if rejection came this time. No excuses. But rejection didn't come. Within a few days I got the word that, yes, he wanted to run my essay.

What?

In November 2004, my essay, which was titled by the *Times* "The Chicken's in the Oven, My Husband's Out the Door," ran in the Sunday Styles section. That Sunday, after my babysitter arrived, I walked by myself to the corner store and bought four copies of the paper with a twenty-dollar bill. No change. I went to a café and unfolded the Styles section and there it was: a half a page in the *New York Times*. My byline. *Mine.*

The words I'd written in the isolation of failure, the words I'd written only for myself, had flown away from me. I'd struggled and pushed to publish *Light Sleeper* and that never came to pass, but these far more honest words had taken off and were now floating around the world, living a life of their own out of my reach.

1. List times when you felt you'd failed in some aspect of your life.

2. Pick one and write about it. As you're writing, try to focus on how that failure led to opportunities that would have been closed to you if you had succeeded the first time around. Were there ways in which that failure led to a later success or, if not success, then maybe an insight (compassion for yourself, maybe) that you could never have gained without that failure?

3. List personal, professional, and creative risks you have taken.

4. List risks you've taken in the last year in any area of your life.

5. If you have long risk lists, pick one risk and write about it. Or write about two risks together.

6. If your risk list is short—especially your list of recent risks— make a list of risks that you might consider taking.

7. Pick one risk from that list.

8. Write down the name of that risk on the top of a piece of paper and then list five things you could do in the next week to prepare to take that risk. For example, call friends for support, visualize taking the risk, research the risk, maybe even take the risk itself.

9. Circle one of these preparatory tasks.

10. Do one of those tasks now.

11. Write for ten minutes on this topic: "What Creative Success Would Look Like to Me."

12. Write for ten minutes on this topic: "How Much Failure Am I Willing to Tolerate to Reach That Success?"

Part Three
Return

13

I Feel So, Uh, Vulnerable

And then it was Monday morning. On Monday morning I wasn't a writer but a mother dropping her kids off at school in a stretched-out sweatshirt. But this particular Monday morning was the first time I would catch the awkward expression of an acquaintance who'd suddenly learned too much about me. It was the face of an acquaintance who'd read about my personal life by pulling the *New York Times* out of its blue plastic bag and unfolding the paper in her well-appointed breakfast nook.

"I read your essay yesterday," she said, blushing. "I wasn't sure if I should be reading it—it seemed so *personal*—but then it was in the newspaper, so I . . . ," she said, her voice trailing off.

The way she said "personal," I instantly understood—whether this was her intention or not—that "personal" was code for "wrong."

"Well, yeah, if it's in the newspaper, it's pretty much fair game, right?" I said goofily. Really, why hadn't I prepared for this moment? What was the protocol here? How is one supposed to handle this weird blurring of the public and private lines? Of course, I should've expected that people would read it and react, and yet somehow I did not anticipate how exposed and vulnerable I would feel.

Often my memoir students will describe themselves as "shy" or "reserved" or as "private people." And while that might seem like a contradiction, I get it. While memoirists might get portrayed as the brashest sort of exhibitionists—the Auntie Mames of the literary world, braggarts overeager to share their most intimate secrets—I've come to believe that's really not the case. Some—perhaps most—of us are, in fact, drawn to memoir because we haven't found another way to express ourselves, because we've never been sure how to come clean about who we are, a step we intuitively understand to be vital to human connection and happiness.

I've always been something of a hider—a hider who can appear to be very confiding and open, at times even confessional, but who's still keeping a few of the key cards tucked away. A hider who's longed to come finally out of hiding.

I'm convinced that every writer has a genre that is her match, a form that is her objective correlative, the literary equivalent of the way she needs to be in the world. Of course, there are writers who can work skillfully in many genres, but I still think there's one genre that matches the note that hums out from a writer's center. Before I found memoir, I wrote autobiographical fiction and autobiographical poems. I longed for memoir before I really understood that it was an option available to me—that I really could write about my own experience without the burden of pretending I was making some or all of it up. I think what I've most wanted from writing all along was, in fact, the very thing that set me on edge that Monday morning: the vulnerability that exposure creates, the "Olly olly oxen free" that calls me out of hiding. And the longer I teach memoir, the more I'm convinced that this yearning to come out is a widely experienced one—that many of us find that the pretense that ordinary life seems to require is one that keeps us isolated.

In the fall of 2005—two years after the demise of *Light Sleeper*—I got my chance to decide how clean I really wanted to come in the world. I got another e-mail from the *Brain, Child* editor who'd interviewed me for the article on the "momoir" publishing trend, this time suggesting that if I ever wanted to send the book out again that I might try her agent, a young up-and-comer.

After a bit of hesitation over the prospect of more rejection, I nudged myself forward. I might as well try, I thought, and sent him the manuscript. He replied quickly that he wasn't interested in *Light Sleeper* (yeah, yeah) but wanted to know what else I had. He really thought I'd have all these manuscripts lying around the house? I told him I just had a few chapters of a memoir about my divorce. The truth was after the first grief-fueled months and the high of the *New York Times* article, my writing had ground to a halt as the idea of churning out another manuscript that would meet who-knows-what fate while trying to make a living and parenting two youngish kids was less than inspiring.

The agent wanted to see the chapters. I sent them. He got

back to me within a day and said that if I wrote up a proposal, he'd have no problem selling it. A proposal for a memoir? That was possible? It was. I wrote it. And ten days later, he sold the proposal in an auction.

Uh.

Because I didn't fully believe the proposal would sell and it all happened so fast, I was stunned to find a book contract in my hand for a book that would be named *How to Sleep Alone in a King-Size Bed*. Even the title seemed crazy personal. *Bed?* Sleeping alone in my bed was the topic for my book? Dear God, what had I done? Yes, I suddenly had the type of success I'd barely dared to hope for, but now I was as terrified as I was excited.

I guess I'll be writing about my divorce then and people will be reading about it, I thought to myself, dread rising. I guess all this was the obvious consequence of writing said proposal and sending it off to an agent, but I wasn't prepared for the book to actually sell. I certainly hadn't been prepared by my experience with *Light Sleeper*, the lesson of which I had presumed to be: Sure, you will toil away writing a very personal book, but never fear—it will never be read by anyone other than a few editors in New York who will skim its opening pages to determine its unworthiness.

But after spending a yummy chunk of the advance—my first purchases were a handheld immersion blender and a nutmeg grinder, which seemed like madcap indulgences—I was able somehow to forget that others would be reading what I wrote and just got busy with the work of writing the book. Over the next year and a half, I kept myself so occupied with writing and editing the book that I was able to ignore the idea that strangers and—worse—people I knew would be reading about some of the most personal and private moments of my life.

Finally, though, the publication loomed. Now every story of people who got in way over their heads—from *Double Indemnity* to *Butch Cassidy and the Sundance Kid*—seemed to be telling my story. I'd once wondered why people who committed major crimes didn't seem to be fully cognizant of the horrific consequences that could befall them. Now it made sense. So *this* is how it happens, I thought almost philosophically, as I shook with fear. It helped, though, to know I wasn't alone. Bernard Cooper expresses this experience perfectly in his brilliant essay "Marketing Memory: Life After Publication," about his own, very similar experience on the eve of the publication of his memoir *Truth Serum*:

> Of course, in the three years it took to write the book, I had deliberately explored personal subject matter. But a good memoir does more than dredge up secrets from the writer's past. A good memoir filters a life through resonant narrative, and in doing so must achieve a balance between language and candor. It was not the subject matter of my memoirs that I hoped would be startling, but rather language's capacity to name what was once nameless, to define what had once been vague and chaotic. The chief privilege of writing a memoir, it seems to me, is the opportunity to go back and make sense of events that left you dumbstruck, mired in confusion, unarmed with the luminous power of words. I'd purposely chosen intimate subjects, not in order to make them public, but because they drove me to probe more

deeply the hidden meaning, imagery and metaphors embedded in memory. Only when the book was on the verge of publication, however, did I realize that this gambit might be treated not as an aesthetic strategy but, rather, as a matter of exhibitionism.

A matter of exhibitionism, indeed.

On the first day of my memoir class every September I pass out a sign-up sheet for the workshops. Without fail, the students fall all over themselves to sign up for the last day of the quarter. And no matter what they claim, it's not *really* because they want more time to work on their pieces. Whenever they workshop, they—being the mortals that they are—will likely still spend approximately the same amount of time on their pieces.

No, the true reason for wanting a delay is terror of exposure and the vulnerability that exposure inevitably forces into bloom.

Sometimes I forget their terror, having sat in the safe seat of the teacher for a few years; but then I remind myself of the workshops in the MFA program, the sensation of exposure that inevitably accompanied the sharing of a story. I felt like a turtle with its shell pried off. During the week in between the distribution of the piece and the workshop, I would obsess over what my professor and classmates must be thinking as they read it.

That feeling of exposure was identical to what I felt on the eve of *King-Size*'s publication. It doesn't matter if the audience is twenty or a few thousand or more. The lizard part of us that holds the fear doesn't bother calibrating the fear based on the number of readers. For Lizard, exposure is exposure: a plain and simple threat to our survival, to the social façade that allows us to hold professional jobs and glide in and out of PTA meetings.

So, if it's a threat, why on earth do we do it?

Because sometimes the safe thing is what's dangerous; sometimes the safe thing puts our happiness at risk. Sometimes the safe thing is suffocating. Sometimes the reward of self-expression is worth the cost of vulnerability.

In the TED lecture "The Power of Vulnerability," researcher and author Brené Brown explains how our happiness, in fact, *depends* on our willingness to make ourselves vulnerable. Even though we might imagine fame, glory, and praise are the tickets to happiness, Brown asserts that the true source of happiness in life lies in our connection to other people. But in order to have that connection, we must be willing to reveal our authentic selves to others. People who believe they are worthy of connection tend to be willing to routinely take that risk and are, as a result of that risk taking, continually reestablishing their connection to others.

So what unravels the connection for so many others? Shame, Brown says. "The one thing that keeps us out of connection is our fear that we're not worthy of love and belonging." She goes on to explain that many of us struggle with the very idea of worthiness. We tend to avoid feeling vulnerable and choose to duck away from opportunities that might reveal our authentic selves. Truly connected and fulfilled individuals—a group whom Brown refers to as "the Wholehearted"—are characterized by a willingness to "fully embrace their vulnerability" and possess "the courage to be imperfect" and therefore are able to experience "connection as a result of authenticity."

Yet, as Tom Petty once said, "even the losers get lucky sometimes." I wouldn't say I'd been living the life of the wholehearted who "fully embraced their vulnerability," but I did back into my vulnerability, and suddenly I was risking more than I ever would have sanely and soberly chosen to risk.

Brown was right. Shame had been keeping me in hiding and it had been doing so all my life. When I was a kid, I was ashamed that I didn't have a dad who saw me more than once a year, and when he did, he greeted me with a casualness that suggested I was a distant relative. Everyone's shame starts somewhere, and mine started with being the dadless girl, no man's special one. My adult life's shame has been that I've been the special one to too many men, that I often picked the wrong partners, and that I've felt like I'm missing the mysterious and essential X factor that makes a relationship endure. Obviously, the child's shame and the adult's shame are connected, but in its grasp, the logic of our shame's origin is of little or no consolation; in the end, we just feel the erosion from the two rivers that have come together to form one.

My shame about my relationship history has kept me out of some important conversations and at one time made me believe there was something essentially flawed about me, something to which I had best not draw too much attention. Tracing this back, I can see that it forced me to miss out on closeness, as I was convinced I wasn't as good or as worthy as some of my friends and acquaintances. Keeping my distance was supposed to protect me from judgment. At a distance, I hoped I would appear as more together than I actually was.

But, for better or for worse, *King-Size* collapsed that distance and forced me out of hiding. Even though most people in the Western world did *not* read this book about my divorce, it felt to me as if they had, which meant I could no longer cling to the delusion that people think I have it together. My image of my social self abruptly changed. There were many moments of awkwardness, including a number of radio interviews in which I was asked to reenact blow by blow the moments that led up to my divorce, as well as clumsy conversations with acquaintances who'd share what point they'd read up to ("Oh, you're just getting back together with your childhood sweetheart!").

Overall, the impact of talking about my divorce publicly was sort of a shock therapy that rearranged the molecules in the place where my shame is stored. The shame that I was a relationship mess case began to diminish, and in what felt like irony to me, this allowed me to feel more connected to more people. I had to admit that my loss looked much like that of others, that my mistakes weren't *that* special, that my shame was, in fact, sadly ordinary. I might still consider myself an outsider, but now I was suddenly aware of how very few of us consider ourselves *insiders*. Alienation, it turns out, is the new black.

TRY THIS

1. Write for ten minutes on whatever comes to mind when you read this quote from Brené Brown: "The one thing that keeps us out of connection is our fear that we're not worthy of love and belonging."

2. List times when you felt ashamed. This is an amazing source of material. If you want to write memoir, go to the shame memories. A beautiful example of memoir material that can come from a personal hall of shame is Lynda Barry's *One Hundred Demons*, one of my all-time favorite books.

3. Pick one of these moments of shame and write it up as a scene, ideally with spoken dialogue, internal dialogue, and descriptions.

4. Repeat step three as often as you can stand it. It's really excruciating at times, I know, but this is where the gold is.

5. Divide your list into Childhood Shame and Adult Shame. What do these lists have in common? How do they differ? That dividing line might just offer the entrance into your memoir material.

6. Brown refers to truly connected and fulfilled individuals who are willing to be vulnerable, imperfect, and authentic as "the Wholehearted." Who are the Wholehearted in your life? Even if you just know them from a distance, add them to your list.

7. Write for ten minutes about one of these wholehearted people. Maybe you'll write a profile of this person or maybe a scene portraying an interaction you had with them in which they revealed their "wholehearted" nature and maybe even their own shame.

14

Someone Loses Something

"Writing is an act of curiosity, of generosity, rather than one of selfishness," Ken Foster says in the introduction to *The KGB Bar Reader*. "Contrary to what we've been taught, there may be just one universal story: Someone loses something."

Someone loses something.

The first time I read this sentence, I was floored by the economy with which it encapsulates the driving force behind the bulk of literature of the past, present, and undoubtedly the future. Most of our stories *are* about loss. Some stories are about finding something after loss, but still Lost trumps Found every time. It's loss we want to know about; it's loss we must learn to endure. As readers, we want to know how the narrator will find her way again after loss. As writers, loss can propel us toward the page, often to write with uncharacteristic abandon. In the rush to get our feelings to the page, we forget ourselves.

It had been the sting of grief that prompted me to take notes in the first days of my marriage's dissolution. Besides my aforementioned bad attitude toward life and publishing, grief fueled my fire as I wrote the early pages of *How to Sleep Alone in a King-Size Bed*. It felt like my misery had to go *somewhere*, and I was already making full use (okay, more than full use) of any friend and family member willing to listen to my misery. I used writing as a means to work through my grief, in part, because I had already established writing as a way to spin meaning out of inchoate suffering. Because in this case I wasn't worried about the end product, I wrote with a rare recklessness. I enjoyed writing then as one enjoys lying down when one is exhausted—because it brings relief. And because I wasn't focused on an audience or the writing's "marketability," those early notes held something raw and powerful, which compelled me to keep writing.

Sometimes unarticulated grief stays lodged in us for a long time—a piece of shrapnel buried between bone and flesh—until it is jarred free. That's what happened to me. In 1989, when I was twenty-seven, I went with my parents on one of my dad's business trips to Japan. He had a ton of frequent-flier miles, so the thinking was that it was "free" to take me, and of course I'd want to go to Japan, right? In my student/waitressing life, I barely had money to go home for visits, let alone foreign travel, so it seemed like I should go anywhere I was taken. Despite all this, however, part of me recognized that not all trips to Japan are created equal and that traveling with my parents would probably never be my first pick.

My family had a long-standing friendship with a woman named Yeiko who had a sort of finishing school for young Japanese adults. We'd met Yeiko through some mutual friends in Vancouver who'd once lived in Japan. Each summer she would bring a group of these students to Vancouver and we would help entertain them. Probably anyone in any culture would feel some need for reciprocity because of that, but add in a traditional Japanese sensibility and the feeling of this woman's perceived indebtedness to us was palpable. During our ten days in Tokyo we were constantly in the custody of one or more of Yeiko's connections, people who showed us the best of Tokyo's *yakatoriyas*, night clubs, and Rodeo Drive–type shopping. Much sushi was eaten; much sake was consumed; a lot of broken English was spoken. We sat around low tables in homes crowded with family, ancient art, and modern electronics. We had no free will of our own and no longer expected to consider our own wants and desires for the duration of our stay in Japan.

I quickly fell into the role of sullen ingrate. Despite the amazing opportunity, I was miserable, as I sometimes am when any reasonable person, it seems, would be happy. I was a broke twenty-six-year-old on a trip with my parents. I hadn't lived at home since I was seventeen and was loath now to play the role of child in my parents' *Who's Afraid of Virginia Woolf?* marriage. Traveling in Japan was not like traveling in Europe, where I might've struck out on my own and maybe figured out the language and how to get home if I got lost. A swirl of fast moving trains, kanji, and a catacomb of identical-looking streets, Tokyo defied comprehension. If I had become accidentally detached from my parents, I would have likely wandered those streets for eternity.

Also, there was something about Japan and its flossy gloss that made me feel dowdy in a way that I never did in San Francisco. One day my escort from Yeiko's entourage was a tiny woman my age in a Chanel suit. She said she worked for CNN as a reporter. At age twenty-seven? Was that *possible*? As she dragged me through Tokyo's glitzy shopping district, I marveled at the disparity between our levels of worldly accomplishment and prestige and wondered how one might take a weekday off from CNN to play tour guide for an awkward American. As much as I told myself, You're in Japan! This is a great opportunity! I longed for my little broke life in San Francisco, to be my own autonomous waitress/grad student self rather than a toddler leashed to my parents and Yeiko's entourage.

One day at the end of the trip, I was signed up for a day of sightseeing in two nearby towns with a group of well-heeled middle-aged Japanese women. The good news was my parents weren't coming, so I could at least semi-pretend that I was an autonomous adult. Plus, I'd much rather spend the day with a group of matronly types than with a hotshot my own age in a Chanel suit. Maybe they'd take care of me, I half imagined, and they did. This group of four women in their forties took on the job of mothering me that day, asking at appropriate intervals if I was hungry, tired, or thirsty, searching through their little dictionaries and then asking me pertinent but not probing questions about my life in San Francisco. Unlike the sullen CNN reporter, these women were prone to fits of laughter and seemed genuinely thrilled to have me as their charge for the day.

We took the train to Yokohama and Kamakura, two neighboring towns an hour or so from Tokyo. As soon as we arrived, I fell in love with Kamakura, a maze of tree-lined streets and old temples and shrines. It was what I'd imagined Japan to be. We walked all around the town, snapping photos and chatting. Then we walked by a temple with open sliding doors. A young Japanese woman in a skirt and sweater kneeled on the hardwood floor. Suddenly, as we passed, she doubled over and let out a howl. A few feet from her, a Buddhist priest in a gray robe spoke to her in a low tone. I was startled by the rawness of her sorrow. Startled but also magnetized. Sensing my reaction, one of my escorts whispered, "She's lost her son, it sounds like."

"Lost?"

"He died."

I looked away from the woman on the floor, not wanting to intrude on her grief. But the honesty of that grief had cut through my center, and as we continued to tour around the town, the primal sound of her sorrow echoed in my head.

After lunch, we arrived at another temple. We walked up a long gravel path lined with hundreds of small stone statues of baby Buddhas with brightly colored bibs tied around their necks. The plastic bibs were incongruous with the stone of the Buddhas and the temple setting.

"What are these?" I asked one of my guides.

"These are called *jizo*s. They're for the babies who've died."

"Oh," I said, thinking briefly of the kneeling woman in the temple and wondering if her son would have a Buddha here.

"Babies who died in miscarriages," she continued, and then added matter-of-factly: "And abortions." She stumbled only slightly on the word "abortions," but it sounded more like a second-language snag than any hesitance about saying the forbidden word out loud. Other than in the news about the war between pro-life and pro-choice, it seemed that I'd rarely heard the word "abortion" spoken aloud, and I couldn't think of a time when I heard the word said so evenly.

"Abortions? I think you might have the wrong word." I didn't want to embarrass her, but I also felt compelled to find out the true purpose of the baby Buddhas.

"No, 'abortion' is right," she said, without hesitation.

"You mean when a woman has an operation when she is pregnant?" I asked, not sure how to phrase it in simple English.

"Yes!" she said.

"Would you mind checking in your dictionary to make sure?" I asked, surprising myself with my own insistence.

"Not at all," she said, flipping through the thin pages. And, then a moment later: "Yes, 'abortion' is right."

"Okay, thank you," I said, not knowing what else to say. She continued up the trail toward the temple that I would later learn was called something that translates roughly as the Temple for Unborn Children, expecting, I'm sure, that I would trail behind her. But I stayed for a few moments with these *jizo*s, and a piece of shrapnel abruptly loosened somewhere deep inside of me.

I fell back in time four years. The Grand Canyon, the Scotch drinking, the snow. The cold day in Santa Fe when a girlfriend had driven me to the abortion clinic, praying there'd be no pick-eters there that day. There'd often been a small group of protest-ers marching back and forth in front of the clinic. But luckily that day they were off scouring the world of evil somewhere else. The day was insanely cold, the sky a blue that can only be achieved in the winter at seven thousand feet. I remembered the barely heated room. Waiting with just the thin paper sheet over me. Waiting, waiting, eternally waiting, eternally cold. And then it was over.

Except it wasn't. I thought it would be over. I thought believ-ing in a woman's right to choose meant I'd leave the abortion there and leave it all behind me. I was twenty-three. I couldn't have been more wrong.

Within a day or so, guilt pierced through me. I hated myself. After a month, I finally gathered up some of my waitressing tips and told a therapist in an old adobe house how I felt. "It's sort of Victorian, don't you think," she said, "to punish yourself with guilt?"

I walked away from the session and never went back. I continued living, dragging a weight of shame with me, never knowing what to do with it. It's a common story, but one rarely portrayed. Other than the old Hemingway story "Hills Like White Elephants" (which never explicitly mentions abortion), I never seemed to come across any stories about abortion, and when I asked a few friends who I knew had had abortions, their experience didn't seem to be quite the same. I knew that part of the problem was that I had so few women I could consult, that in any tiny sample it was uncommon to find people who were troubled by an experience in an identical way. Even then, I suspected that if I could talk to lots of women about this or I could read lots of their stories, I'd find at least a few whose experience more closely resembled my own. But I had no means of accessing these stories. There was no socially acceptable way to bring the question up. And even if there had been, my shame would likely have kept me silent.

With no means of expressing my grief, I pushed it down and down. What did it matter that I no longer wanted to have sex unless I was half-drunk? What did it matter that I felt like I'd betrayed someone but could never quite name who? What did it matter if I flinched whenever my memory strayed that way?

But now, standing in front of the temple, I felt something— a shift. It wasn't just a reaction to the sweet stone *jizo*s looking beatifically forward into the future with their poignant plastic bibs secured under their chins. It was also the straightforward voice with which the woman had said they were for miscarriages and abortions. No shame, no hush. Just "And abortions." They count. They get commemorated. You don't have to just push it away. These solid stone babies insisted to the world that abortion existed and that a baby lost that way was worth recognizing. That *I* was worth recognizing. That the abortion and I didn't exist in a netherworld beyond the reach of humanity and spirit. The *jizo*s seemed to speak: we lived, we died, and we forgive you.

Somehow that woman's simple voicing of the unsaid within the gaze of the stone *jizo*s had broken the spell. The grief, the guilt, the shame, they were still there, yes, but halved in mass and weight in a reduction so swift and dramatic that I felt certain that they would eventually be gone, if not completely, then almost.

My grief had stayed stashed within me until it found another form to fill, a means of existing in the world outside of me, a means of expression. "When we tell our own stories, we are forgiven," I heard someone say recently. Upon first hearing this, I thought briefly, Forgiven for what?—and now the answer, for me at least, is clear: for being human.

My friend Abigail Carter seems to agree. "When we tell our own stories in an honest way, we give permission to others to tell their stories honestly as well," she told me on a recent rainy Seattle evening, sitting in a crowded bar. "You are freeing people to be authentic by telling your story honestly, courageously."

"What are you free of?" I asked.

"Guilt. Shame. Feeling disconnected from the world."

I met Abby in January 2006 in the very first section of my memoir writing course at the University of Washington. I noticed her right away, a pretty woman in her early forties sitting in the back row. When I saw her there, I thought (I'm not sure why): Something's wrong. She's a happy person who for some reason is very sad.

I pushed the thought aside and then remembered it when she handed in her first workshop piece, a story about some of her first dates as a widow. Her husband had been at a breakfast meeting at Windows on the World on September 11. Abby was thirty-five in 2001, with a six-year-old daughter and a two-year-old son. A year or so after that, Abby, who'd never considered herself a writer, began to think about writing about her surreal experience of her husband's sudden death and the crazy events that followed that, including, among other things, meeting Prince Charles and the Prime Minister of Canada and attending a public memorial for the families at Ground Zero.

"I held myself up for two years, though, trying to define what I should write: a book for kids? For widows?" Abby says. "As a result, I didn't write anything until my therapist suggested that perhaps it didn't matter what I wrote, that just getting it down was what was important. Best advice ever. I sat down just after returning from England, where we went for the second anniversary of 9/11, and wrote 'September 11th, 2001' across the top of the page and started writing."

Without a plan or permission from anyone to write or "be a writer," Abby had forged ahead. "That first write was sort of a 'vomit' of words. I just wrote. I had no idea what I was doing. It was really an exercise in memory for me at that point. I didn't worry about grammar or spelling. Sometimes I had to check with people who were at a particular event, because my memory of the early days of widowhood was pretty sketchy. I just wrote whenever I could, story by story—or bird by bird, as Anne Lamott would say, though I didn't know who she was at the time."

From watching Abby's process, I learned that grief can create a great need to write, to form a story, and that in the very telling of the story, the grief slowly, gradually begins to lift. Just over a year after I met Abby, her book was published in Canada, and then in the U.S., Australia, and the Netherlands. Through writing *The Alchemy of Loss: A Young Widow's Transformation*, Abby became connected to widows, widowers, and others besieged by grief all over the world. She began speaking to groups about loss and healing and connected with even more readers through her blog. The loss that had brought her to the page had transformed into a book that, in turn, transformed her life.

I've seen this process repeated with students and other writers many times. Many of the students who take my class would never have dreamed of taking a writing class before living through a trauma—often the loss of someone essential to their lives—which resulted in a great need to express their experience. Grief seems to override a person's self-consciousness as a writer. Like Abby, these writers find that the need to express what they've been through is greater than their fear that they're not up to the task.

And for those already established as writers, writing can be a first port of refuge when loss blows through their lives. It wasn't long after her son, Jason, was killed in the Battle of Wanat in Afghanistan that my friend Carlene Cross, author of *Fleeing Fundamentalism: A Minister's Wife Examines Faith* and *The Undying West: A Chronicle of Montana's Camas Prairie*, took to the page. Two years after Jason died in 2008, Carlene had finished a screenplay about the Battle of Wanat, and now she's working on a memoir about her experience of surviving her son. Like Abby, Carlene says that the initial words she wrote about Jason's death came out of her in a rush and that she would spend hours holed up with her computer, typing through the tears at times but continuing nonetheless. "I felt like Jason was telling me to keep going," Carlene says.

Teaching my memoir class over the last six years has been a lesson in humility. Each year in September, I face a classroom of strangers, and by June I say good-bye to a group of people whose stories of loss have become as familiar to me as those of my close friends. No matter how unscathed by life these students may have seemed to me in the fall, by the end of each year my assumptions about the ease of their lives have been dashed. Every year I am reminded that the story of loss is indeed our universal story and the need to find expression for that story is essential to our humanity.

1. Answer this question very quickly in list form and include the abstract as well as the concrete: What have you lost? Things, people, preconceptions, dreams, hopes, fears—include them all.

2. Which losses have you not yet recovered from?

3. Write for ten minutes on a loss from which you have recovered. As you're writing, think about what aided your recovery.

4. On a day when you think you're ready, write for twenty minutes on a loss from which you have *not* recovered. You might want to plan a pleasant and distracting activity to do after this writing session, such as talking to a friend or watching a comedy.

5. Write about a loss you didn't know how to grieve or that has been difficult to articulate.

15

Memoir: It's All About You

(and the Rest of Us)

A lot of my writing ideas come in the night. Four a.m. It's not so much that I dream an idea as I'm washed up onto a shore where there are no ideas. Once my mind is quiet, then an idea comes: Write about this. Now go turn on the light.

But sometimes, very rarely, an actual idea comes in a dream. I had one such dream a few years ago. It is exceedingly boring to hear a recounting of another's dreams. I understand that it's up there with the recounting of acid trips. So, briefly, here's the up-shot: I was in an art gallery. The show was all self-portraits. One piece was simply three typed pages on a podium. When I asked a faceless person about this piece, they said it was a portrait of the artist's life that he'd written in twenty-six minutes.

Eyes open. Light on. Capture the essence of your life in twenty-six minutes. Yes! I grabbed a notepad and a pen. I looked at the clock. Six eleven a.m. (not four a.m.—nice). I wrote for twenty-six minutes. The piece I wrote was about being alone and how being alone was a recurring thread that ran throughout my life. I liked what I wrote. But more than that, I liked the exercise. I liked the idea of trying to get to the essence of one's existence in a very short time frame, with no warning, no recourse, no planning, no extra time. That evening I told my class about the 26-Minute Memoir. They were intrigued. The cool part was they didn't question it too much. Write about the theme of your life in twenty-six minutes—okay. So we set the timer. They wrote. They liked it, and many of them kept working with the pieces they'd begun in that twenty-six-minute frame. To give you an idea of the possibilities of the form, here is one of the 26-Minute Memoirs written that night, this one by my student Natalie Singer:

As much as the house I grew up in, the cars my parents drove, the cold classrooms and school hallways I roamed for years—as much and more as these touchstones, when I think of my childhood, I think of the mall.

I can see myself there now, standing at the end of the low brown, brick building, under a dull flickering fluorescent.

I have just walked through the glass doors near the entrance to Eaton's, the Canadian department store where we bought our boots and underwear and where, in its heyday as an upper-class destination, my grandparents had taken me to lunch at the cafeteria. I still feel the cheese lasagna steaming my eager little face, my Mary Janes knocking the post underneath the laminate table.

But now I am 14. It is snowing outside, the big new flakes of another winter. My hair is puffy, my coat is wide open, a plain gray school uniform rumpled underneath. I am walking with a couple of girlfriends, gossiping about boys or the bitchy geography teacher. But even as I nod and swear perfunctorily, I am fielding my own private thoughts.

We walk past the windows of the stores, Jacob, Roots, Mexx. I study the mannequins, who are wearing the kind of clothes that I don't own. They pose in their short black skirts, leather boots, bomber jackets. I cannot have these things, because they cost money my mother doesn't have.

I marvel at the mannequins' smoothness, their creamy unblemished robot skin. I am the opposite of them, me with my frumpy sweater from Reitman's, where the mothers and cleaning ladies shop, where my own mother drags me when I desperately need something new and berates me. "What is wrong with this?" she asks, urges, waving a polyester thing in my face. "You are so spoiled. Money doesn't grow on trees. And I don't see your father offering to buy you kids anything."

When the mannequins become too much, I turn my focus to the other groups of girls and boys my age roaming the grubby mall floor in little cliques. I pass right by some of them but they do not look, as though I am the air itself.

These girls seem to defy their very DNA—they almost all attend the private Jewish day schools nearby. But they are crowned with shiny gold hair, glossy and straight down their backs or gathered in sexy/messy ponytails jutting out the back of their small, well-shaped heads. They wear uniforms too, but their skirts have sharp, black pleats, their tights patterned, their boots laced high. They have diamonds in their ears and gold nameplates hanging down their neck.

These girls, who sometimes knock into me as they brush by, walk with boys. Beautiful, unreal boys with longish hair and letter jackets and white teeth. Boys who put their arms around the girls and grip their small waists. Boys to whom I am invisible.

I stand in my puffy, gaping coat and study the mall floor tiles as these kids move by, as though I have important business down there and my ears aren't red. This is how it is for me, how it always has been. I am fine—I look ok, not beautiful but not horrifically ugly, a little pimply but not covered from chin to forehead in fat blackheads like Andrea Betamun in homeroom. I know the requirements for fitting into the world around me—stylish clothes like the mannequins, glossy hair, manicured nails. But I don't have the key to get in. I can't get through those windows. I need to be perfect, I know that, but I can't.

So I walk with my other invisible friends through the mall, past the colored cement indoor playground my grandparents took me to as a child, past the deli where the bubbies in their fur coats order challah and eggplant spread, past the Cattleman's where the glossy girls and sometimes me stop for wide golden steak fries stacked like thick pencils in their oily paper cups.

The voices of the mall travel and echo like a train station, muffled, a sort of engine revving to take off. I am here, but not a part of anything. The thrum of the mall, as with life outside its walls, moves past me. I stand in place and watch it go, feeling slightly drugged, unable to keep up with the action, the requirements. I think about the walk to my bus stop, the icy wait, trudging through the slush piled up on the sidewalk, the cracked steps leading up to our sagging duplex.

I think about the other girls, ponytails, gliding up their pillared walkways into golden lit hallways and sitting rooms painted red. In my loose-fitting coat, in the middle of the brown mall, I am cold. Cold and unperfect. And, as usual, alone.

I marvel at Natalie's ability here to arrive at the essential story so quickly. I can't help but think that the urgency of the twenty-six-minute assignment helped free her to write such a compelling and honest scene rich with exquisitely particular details. After seeing my students' pieces that night, I became hooked on twenty-six minutes for a while. When I'd sit down to write, I'd write for twenty-six-minute stretches. I started proselytizing about the virtues of the twenty-six-minute writing assignment, trying to see if I could bring others into this new way of life I'd created. I wondered if there were some inherent magic in the number 26. I added the numbers and divided them.

I started a blog called 26 Minutes (now housed at Writing IsMyDrink.com) and asked Facebook friends, strangers—anyone—to set the timer, write, and then send me their unedited pieces. I trusted that they wouldn't go past the time (it's not like there's a huge incentive to "cheat") and that they wouldn't edit and that they wouldn't send anything that I wouldn't feel comfortable posting. To date, I've published all the 26-Minute Memoirs that people have submitted to me, and I have to say, I love them. There is a rawness and vitality to them that I find remarkable. And writers have told me that they've had a great deal of fun writing them. There are now many 26-Minute Memoirs posted at WritingIsMyDrink.com; some writers have even written more than one 26-Minute Memoir. If you'd like to write a 26-Minute Memoir of your own and submit it to be posted, please do (details for submitting are in the "Try This" exercise at the end of this chapter).

And what I started to notice in reading these memoirs written in twenty-six minutes is that they tended to have an arc—that for the most part they charted the course of a transformation, even if it was something as subtle as a shift in perception, a new insight into an old story. When Claire Dederer, the author of the *New York Times* best seller *Poser: My Life in Twenty-three Yoga Poses*, came to visit my class recently, she articulated something of crucial importance about the arc of a memoir: "Thinking the event is the story is the biggest mistake of student writers of memoir," Dederer said. "The transformation of the self is the story."

As I hurried to scribble this down, two things scrolled across my thoughts: the majesty of Vivian Gornick's *The Situation and the Story: The Art of the Personal Narrative* and the latest *New York Times* piece in the paper's continuing effort to eradicate memoir as a literary form.

First, let's talk about Gornick. In the slim but mighty tome *The Situation and the Story*, Gornick asserts that in personal narrative the plot itself is not *the story*. The story is the magic the writer creates out of the events, the brew of insight, metaphor, and voice that renders the events meaningful. In fact, here's exactly what she said: "Every work of literature has both a situation and a story. The situation is the context or circumstance, sometimes the plot; the story is the emotional experience that preoccupies the writer: the insight, the wisdom, the thing one has come to say."

"*The emotional experience that preoccupies the writer.*" That phrase articulates perfectly what I find most compelling in memoir. I'm not so much interested in the events the narrator has endured as I am in the narrator's insight into the experience. There are all sorts of crazy life stories out there, but to me what's interesting is what the story *means* to the writer. And that brings me to the aforementioned *New York Times* article.

A few months before Claire's visit to my class, I'd received a flurry of e-mails from my students one Sunday afternoon: "Have you seen this?" they asked. I could almost see their ashen faces as I read the article attached, titled ominously, "The Problem with Memoirs." One of my e-mailers wrote: "I just pictured a million writers shutting down their laptops simultaneously." The *Times* piece—and it's by no means an isolated one—was all about how we don't need any more of these crappy memoirs that are clogging the bookstore shelves.

As I read the review, I was instantly of two minds: The first: Forget you, Mr. Smug Reviewer of Books who has probably never dared to enter into the sweaty arena of writing about one's own experience. The second: Yes, actually I think you might be right. There *is* a type of memoir I do find a bit flat. For me, it's the type of memoir that editor Rachel Klayman once summed up as "a forced march through the writer's life."

"A forced march" is another way of saying that the writer has mistaken the events for the story. Obviously, this is easiest to do when the events of the writer's life are dramatic. It's easy, say, to believe that the stories of a traumatic childhood or the journey to alcoholism's bottom and back are in themselves enough. But I think it goes back to what Mary Karr said about "sound bite memoirs" that recount every instance of a mother's abuse and overlook the real story, which lies in the fact that no matter how much the narrator was abused, his real problem is that he still loves his mother. Which reminds me of Dederer and her insight that the transformation of the self is the story. And for me, this transformation-of-the-self story is the type of memoir I want *more* of, and it tends to come in two forms: memoirs that take a quiet situation like *Poser*'s (a new mother pursues yoga) and render it into a story that speaks volumes about something larger than the narrator (in *Poser*'s case: the women's movement, the impact of divorce, the state of middle-class motherhood) and memoirs in which the narrator goes to the mat with the fact that despite abuse love endures.

There was something else that troubled me about the *New York Times* "Problem with Memoirs" article: its willingness to buy into wholesale memoir-as-less-important-literary-form snobbery. To identify overlooked sexism, Gloria Steinem often offers a substitution. The sexism of dumb-blonde jokes, say, is exposed if the word "black" or "Latino" were to be subbed in for the word "blonde." Taking a cue from Steinem, I can't help but see that if the word "novels" were subbed in for the word "memoirs" in the headline, "The Problem with Memoirs," the bias against the memoir genre on the part of the reviewer, the *Times*, and the reading public comes sharply into focus. It's absurd to think of an essay with the title "The Problem with Novels" because we generally accept that the novel is a varied, inherently valuable, and irremovable literary form, a form about which few blanket statements can be made and one that no reasonable modern-day reviewer would ever suggest that we need no more of—a form that, while often autobiographical, we do not tend to think of as inherently narcissistic or "navel-gazing."

But the memoir? The memoir is fair game. The memoir, routinely belittled, is a sort of embarrassment, a literary form that any scribbler can create and that is somehow a symptom of the worst of our culture's narcissism. It is the Kardashian of the literary forms. To be a writer of memoir is to be forever a little flushed in the face, a little squeaky in answering the question "What do you write?"

While writers of every conceivable literary form from the haiku to the screenplay draw from their own experience for inspiration and content, the memoirist is the most exposed; the promise that the story told is based exclusively on her own experience makes her especially vulnerable to scrutiny and, for some reason, derision.

The snobbery seems to rest on the perception of the memoir as *merely* the retelling of experience without the filter of imagination and on the assumption that the writer of memoir is more self-involved than other writers who fold imagined ingredients into the mix. Imagination, it would seem, is the elevating literary element. When *memoirists* have used their imaginations, however, this we do not like at all—and for legitimate reasons. We want memoirists to stick to factual accounts of their lives, but we also want the pleasure of snubbing them and insinuating that their work is a mere recording of events, a sort of transcription activity that anyone with a laptop and the will to write can pull off. But the truth is much imagination *is* required in the writing of memoir—not the imagination needed to conjure events or characters, but the imagination required to take a series of personal experiences and forge them into a coherent story that illuminates a universal experience.

Interestingly, the maligned memoir genre tends to be the literary form with which women have enjoyed a great deal of success. It is also a form that tends to be more compelling to women readers and writers than to their male counterparts. Just saying.

Maybe some of this backlash is just growing pains. Having become a recognized genre in the mid-nineties with books like *Angela's Ashes*, *This Boy's Life*, *The Liars' Club*, and *An American Childhood*, the contemporary memoir is just now heading out of a rough, identity-searching adolescence. The James Frey debacle represented, perhaps, the drunken grad party the police had to break up. No longer scattered across the bookstore and mashed into the biography section, memoir finally has a shelf of its own. People recognize memoir when they see it. No one says *mem-WAHs* with a French accent anymore.

Although the nineties witnessed the first wave of memoir as a publishing phenomenon, the force that created the genre originated in the humanist movements of the 1960s and 1970s: namely, the civil, women's, and gay rights movements, which fostered a climate in which people met in church basements or around someone's kitchen table and said to each other "This is what it was like for me" and received the nod of recognition from each other, the "Amen" that says your coming-out story, your story of discrimination, your story of abuse has been heard. Your secret personal story has been heard and now lives in the public domain, where it can be seen for what it is: a retelling of the universal experience of the individual seeking transformation, release, redemption, and a place in the world. Today memoir offers us a place to express stories we have no other means to fully express—stories that often tell the tales of isolation, abuse, and recovery. And the fact that we stand by our stories with the stamp of "nonfiction" that the label "memoir" carries gives the reader an assurance that neither the writer nor the reader who sees her experience mirrored in the story is just "making it up." Those surreal circumstances that you sometimes question—*Did that really happen?*—they are, in fact, real. In reading and writing memoir, we bear witness to each other's lives in a culture in which we have become simultaneously more visible in ways that don't count and less visible in the ways that truly matter. Our every movement conceivably could be documented on social media, and yet our grief, isolation, and fear are the stories we keep locked away in increasingly remote hiding places.

Memoir offers companionship through what surely must be one of the loneliest moments in the history of civilization. Lisa Jones, author of the memoir *Broken: A Love Story*, describes the role of the memoirist like this: "You're simply a nice carpenter who has helped make a shelter for other people's uneasiness by exposing your own." No matter how important we are, how busy our schedules, how big our houses, we all still need comfort and shelter. From each other's stories, we learn how to endure heartbreak, to feel connected, to survive, and to thrive. The stories that were once routinely told around the fire, the kitchen table, the living room, we need them still.

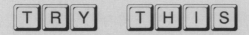

1. Go to WritingIsMyDrink.com/26Minutes and read examples of the 26-Minute Memoir.

2. Set the timer for twenty-six minutes. Write without stopping with the idea in mind that you are trying to capture the essence of your life. There is no right or wrong here. Some 26-Minute Memoirs describe one specific scene and others describe a lifetime. Let yourself be free to go wherever the writing takes you.

    Try not to stop to correct or edit. If you pause to let the ideas come, that's fine. This assignment should be something like a freewriting: Keep writing without stopping for twenty-six minutes. It can be handwritten or typed. Writers learn quite quickly which method works best for them, and many switch back and forth between writing by hand and working on the computer. (I tend to start all writing projects with my fine-tip black Sharpie and a yellow legal pad. Once I feel like I've got a good footing on a piece, I'll switch over to the computer.) Find the method that works best for you.

    When the twenty-six minutes are up, read over your piece. What are you excited about here? Are there any ideas here that you want to keep developing?

    If you're interested in publishing your 26-Minute Memoir on the Writing Is My Drink blog, e-mail me at theonestor@gmail.com.

3. Keep paper and pen on your nightstand. If you get a writing idea in the middle of the night, write it down.

4. Make up a writing exercise of your own. If it feels like a vital idea, consider making a blog based on the writing exercise and ask others to contribute. WordPress and Blogger blogs are very easy to set up.

5. Make a list of memoirs that are important to you.

6. Pick a memoir from the list and flip through it again to identify how the narrator transforms during the story. How does the narrator evolve from the first page of the book to the last? How does the writer bring that transformation to life on the page?

7. If you are currently working on a memoir or personal essay, try to identify in a sentence or two how the narrator changes over the course of the piece. Remember that the transformation can be a very subtle one, but there must be some sort of change in the narrator by the end of the piece.

16

The Art of Lolling, Lounging, and Loafing

Here's the thing: If you're going to write, you're going to need to do some hard-core lolling, lounging, and loafing. You're going to be lying on the bed, staring at the ceiling. You'll be lying on the sofa, staring into the fire. Sometimes you'll be sitting in the sand, staring slack-jawed at the incoming surf. You're going to be *wasting time*—or at least it looks a lot like wasting time. And if you're not completely comfortable with that—and frankly, only half of me is—you will feel guilty when you are writing as well as guilty when you are not. Welcome to my world.

"How's the time wasted?" you ask. It isn't *truly* wasted, but it will have the appearance of waste to both yourself and others. Time will seem to be squandered during the crazy gestation period in which you aren't quite ready to write and yet you can't quite be out and about, doing other things that feel more "real," because any minute you might be ready to write.

Or maybe you won't waste time. Maybe you're not like me. Maybe you're one of those people who just sits down and does it. Good for you! But me, before I start a new chapter, a new essay, any new project, I need to do this lolling, this chaise lounging, this wave watching, this autistic rocking.

Let's take today. It's the Saturday of Labor Day weekend. Now, holiday weekends have always been a special struggle for me, because I feel I should be doing the BIG-ticket activities that people are prone to on these weekends: outdoor music festivals (too crowded, too loud), lake boating (um, no boat), and camping (life's hard enough; why turn it into a three-ring circus by trying to rub sticks together just so you can boil water for morning coffee?). And while I love good weather as much as the next person, I am often enjoying good weather from the great indoors or from a sheltered balcony a few yards from fridge, kettle, and my own bed.

Today I am on said balcony, lolling on the chaise, getting ready to write. I've eaten a bowl of Rocky Road ice cream, finished the cold remains of my coffee, and watched the heartbeat of a spiderweb pulse in the breeze. Any eyewitness could tell you no work is happening here, and yet . . . and yet it is. I cannot begin a new piece of writing without the "pre-writing lolling." Believe me, I've tried. So, this is work. Work that—to the untrained eye or to the eyes of just about anyone over the age of five—is the very image of loafing.

In these scheduled-to-the-teeth times, it's an act of defiance to call loafing "work" or even to spend time earmarked as leisure lolling and scribbling notes on a yellow legal pad. But every movie we watch, every book we read, every song on the radio, started out as someone's scribble somewhere. And before there was the scribble, I'm betting, in many cases, there was the loll. In a culture that favors any type of activity, no matter how silly (shopping for dog sweaters, playing slot machines, TiVoing reality shows) or destructive (invading small nations, roaring all-terrain vehicles over fragile ecosystems), reclining on a chaise and staring at a spider's web can feel like a war crime.

Maybe that's why if I have enough days filled with errands, housework, and bill-paying work, I'm prone to dangerous thinking. It's a type of thinking that is akin to a lust, a lust for a certain type of groovy, hippie writing feeling. And like many forms of lust, this one is built on a fantasy and is merely an escape from the real work of a relationship, in this case my relationship with the reality of my ordinary divorced mom/writing life.

So my Walter Mitty thinking looks something like this: If only I could be in a certain hippie place under certain groovy conditions, I would once again get that groovy, hippie writing feeling and effortlessly fill pages with authentic and seamless prose.

The thing is I *have* had these Super Writing Days a few times, and unfortunately these certain stunning locales and bohemian conditions do seem to have inspired them, which leads me to this fantasy that if I could just return to one of those places, I would have another Super Writing Day.

My Super Writing Days have come reliably in semirural

settings where urban hippie types have transported themselves with good coffee and a certain sensibility for art and music in tow. On more than one occasion I've had Super Writing Days at the Teahouse on Canyon Road in Santa Fe—yes, that's right, a mere 1,500 miles from my Seattle home.

The Teahouse is nestled (really, nestled; people say "nestled" when they mean "near," but this really is a case of big-"N" Nestled) in the base of the Sangre de Cristo Mountains up a long, sometimes dusty road of art galleries. The Teahouse is an old adobe house of several rooms of cool white walls and pristine hardwood floors. Outside the Teahouse, it is perpetually 80 degrees and inside it is perpetually 70 degrees with a subtle cross breeze flowing between the two opposing screen doors. Although I would not normally listen to Bob Marley, in the Teahouse his music seems just right and is perpetually playing (sometimes alternating with songs that evoke nostalgia for the best parts of youth and yet promise a sort of sophisticated life that can only be purchased with a post-youth salary, such as Cyndi Lauper's "Time After Time" covered by Miles Davis). This music plays at a perfect volume, which allows you to be moved by the music when you choose to be aware of it and also to forget it's playing when you fall into concentration. You are being quietly indoctrinated into a world where getting to the beach or the bistro is the tallest order of the day. Or maybe just working in a perfect flow state on that involving but not overly taxing writing project. Sandaled and slightly reverential but not fawning androgynous waiters bring coffee and then, later, a lunch menu. They do not care that you will seemingly be staying for the rest of time at Table 12. They believe in you and your work and do not resent you because they are not working on their one-person shows or large abstract canvases at this moment. Is there Wi-Fi? you ask. Yes, there is, but that's of little consequence to you now as you fill page after page. You have your hippie writing groove on now, and your only thought for the future is how you will return here tomorrow.

The Teahouse is a place where the need to loll, lounge, and loaf is understood. It's a place where wasted time is time well spent, but there's the irony. In the Teahouse, the need for the loll is not so pressing because the Teahouse environment provides the loll state of mind for me. Surrounded by the lackadaisical, I no longer need to create a buffer zone between the bustle-bustle of life and my writing world.

The longer I go without a good writing day, the more susceptible I am to the Teahouse Fantasy. If only I could get to the Teahouse or another similarly groovy location, then I would write without struggle and false starts, I am sure of it. But let's say I did go there and I did have those Super Writing Days; I would still come home again. Home of orthodontist appointments (so many appointments) and teens texting about forgotten lunches and rides needed. Home of my cluttered desk and long to-do list. And home—no matter what might happen on fantasy junkets—is where most of a book must be written. And so here I am at home, showing up for my slow-thinking mind and pages of false starts. But after enough slow thoughts and false starts, the pace will quicken; it always does. And then it won't matter where I am.

1. Write for ten minutes about wasting time. What's your family's view on wasting time? In most cases, it's pretty grim, but most people are wasting much more time than they're willing to admit and not even getting to creative activities. How willing are you to waste time? To spend a day thinking, or dreaming? Scary stuff.

2. Set aside a day when nothing can be scheduled. A secular Sabbath. A day when you can do whatever you want. Some of you are thinking: Big deal, I do that all the time. But many others have not had a completely unscheduled day for as long as they can remember. If this is you, you may find this unnerving. But I think it's a worthwhile challenge. By clearing space in our schedules, we allow a type of thinking that doesn't occur in short spaces; we allow our minds to stretch out into a wide open landscape.

3. Challenge: Schedule a day when nothing can be scheduled that is also an Internet holiday. That's right: your time and your thoughts to yourself all day.

17

Words, Fail Me Not

Just as there is no way to become a published writer without having been a rejected writer, there is no way to write anything good without having written stuff that is truly bad. And that's just one of the many things about writing that always scares me witless—scares me enough to keep me away.

It's a trick, this continual talking myself down, this persuading myself back to the page. Somehow I do it, but the monsters never go away for good. What I've learned, though, is that almost every writer seems to have a set of demons of his own.

It seems there's no banishing the demons, so then we're left living with them. Naming them seems to help me. So I will call my demons out from under the bed and introduce you to them. Maybe you'll know a few.

#1: *The Platonic Ideal*

I squandered much of my youth half-learning a lot of important ideas, and this has gotten me into trouble. Sometimes, a couple of half-learned ideas will get snagged in my mind, whirl around in there, and gel into the shape of a potent tormentor. One of these tormentors was born when I was introduced to the Platonic ideal in Philosophy 101. This is the idea—as I half-learned it—that the things that inhabit this earth are mere shadowy representations of their ideal forms, which exist . . . somewhere. I think in a cave. Like I said, I half-learned it. And while I don't claim to understand it, somehow this sliver of knowledge stayed in my mind. By itself it's not that dangerous, just a whisper of a poorly comprehended piece of philosophy. But then, within a few years, my brain's version of the Platonic ideal crossed paths with a quote. And when those two came together, a nuclear meltdown occurred that still radiates damage decades later.

The quote is from Michelangelo: "In every block of marble I see a statue as plain as though it stood before me, shaped and perfect in attitude and action. I have only to hew away the rough walls that imprison the lovely apparition to reveal it to the other eyes as mine see it."

You can probably see where this is headed. Sometime right after the cold fusion of these two bits of knowledge, I came up with this tormented belief: For any story—short story, article, novel, memoir, what have you—there is an Ideal Story, a perfect way to tell that story. And my task is to uncover that story, to write it the way it was *meant to be told*. Yes, that's right, apparently there's a divine order of storytelling, and stories are meant to be told one ideal way. A writer's job is simply to "hew away the rough walls" and release this ideal story as Michelangelo released his sculptures: "I saw the angel in the marble and carved until I set him free."

So what does this belief in that Platonic ideal of the Story mean for me? The first symptom is that I am very apprehensive to begin a writing project—even a very small one, an essay, a chapter (yes, even the chapter you're reading now)—for fear of botching the start. Because, a botched start must surely be the starting point of missing the mark for the ideal. Couldn't you just start over? you ask. In theory, yes, but once the botched start is under way, you've created a motion that was intended to carry you to the end of the story, chapter, or what have you. And according to my partially learned Newton: Once that motion has begun, it takes on a life and existence of its own. It has a destiny as a story that will forever be in conflict with the destiny of what would have been.

It's the genie that won't pop back into the bottle.

So, yes, you can imagine how eager I am to start new writing projects! I love believing that if I blow the beginning, the project will be destroyed beyond repair, even if I ball up the paper, tear it up, or wipe out all evidence of that missed-mark start with the delete key.

But even when I start out okay and it doesn't feel like a botch, there are still a million missteps I can take, right? So the worry hangs out on my shoulder as I proceed.

The good news: Once I'm past a certain point—usually midway—I often become convinced myself that somehow I have stumbled onto the story As It Was Meant to Be Told.

Why is this totally messed up? The thinking here is so flawed, it's hard to know where to begin, but first let's say this: The joy in writing is the adventure of finding where the story will take you. If there were some static ideal it was my job to unearth, I think I'd have little interest in being the digger. Writing is smarter than all of us. The way a story will evolve is wildly unpredictable, and it's in that unpredictability that most of us find something that's actually good (meaning it speaks to others). There is no ideal. We are not chipping away to the angel underneath. Instead, we are meeting the angel on the road and wrestling like Jacob. If we come out alive, we have a story.

When I was a kid, I was petrified of clowns. And once, when JoJo took me to a parade, I gasped when I remembered about the clowns and looked over at her in the driver's seat and asked, "What about the clowns?"

"Just keep telling yourself 'Clowns can't hurt me' when they walk by."

And that's exactly what I did: I sat there on the curb muttering "Clowns can't hurt me" over and over, and I got through— even perhaps enjoyed—the parade.

So now I have to tell myself—and maybe you do, too—that false starts can't hurt me. False starts can't hurt me. False starts can't hurt me. Because, really, they can't.

So that's our first demon.

#2: I Will Die All Alone Here and No One Will Find My Body in This Sealed Tomb Known As Writing

For me, starting to work is a bit like diving into cold water. I can hover over the edge of the pool all day, and I can't make myself fall into a dive. It might as well be a pit of snakes. For me, work feels binary. Either you're in—in the deep end, swimming madly—or you're on the couch. Or playing Scrabble online. And no matter how many times I've learned the lesson that I really do like writing, working, swimming, I still feel this aversion to starting. I feel like I'm giving up free will. Once I'm in, I'll be buried alive and unable to make contact with the outside world. Just that. Just buried alive. No biggie.

So naturally, when you're facing the prospect of being buried alive, the warm-up time can be long. Another cup of coffee. Checking e-mail one more time. Maybe just run out and check the mail. Start dinner? Go to the store? And sometimes, I actually never start writing that day, and my brain remembers those days, and because it can remember, my brain is fully aware of the escape hatch, and the devil within strokes his goatee and says, "You know, this doesn't always end in writing. I'm not sure this won't be one of *those* days. One of those days when you never *quite* make it. You just squander your time. You know, you could actually be doing something fun right now?"

But if I can make it past the electric fence that surrounds work, I usually make it. Often I have to trick myself in. For some reason, if I start by handwriting in the margins of a copy of whatever I'm working on, I can get myself to work, telling myself that this isn't writing; I'm just making a few notes. I usually work, even if it's just a little. Some writing gets done, and then after a little while, most of the time, it happens: I'm under and swimming madly.

#3: *I Don't Have Time for This!*

Have I mentioned that I'm behind? I'm behind right now. I'm a youngest child, born on the cusp of my parents' divorce. Talk about being behind: I totally missed the party five years earlier—the boating, the patio parties, the Camelot days of my family. Around age five I clued in that something good had happened before I arrived and I'd missed it. It's okay. I'm fine, except for this lingering feeling of trying to catch up.

I tend to have two speeds, frantic running and paralysis, neither super-conducive to writing. Not long ago, I was at my mother's and I found a Post-it stuck to the windowsill in the kitchen with just one word: Hurry! When I asked my mom about this, she said she felt like she doesn't get enough done in a day, so she posted this reminder to herself. Oooo-kay, I thought. Now I know where I learned the frantic running.

But I strive to work sometimes at what I think of as the Third Speed, the one I assume is employed by government workers everywhere: a speed of relaxed paddling, in which a reasonable but not astonishing amount of work gets done over an eight-hour stretch at a fairly consistent rate punctuated by periods of sloth spent hanging over the cubicle partition or resting with one's forehead on the desk. One can write an essay in frantic running mode. Just sit down, hold your breath, and write it. But for longer projects, you've got to be able to work at the Third Speed and try to avoid the frantic running, which tends to end in bouts of paralysis. During the frantic times, I'm consumed with the idea that I don't have time to do everything I have to do, and so ironically I become paralyzed and do nothing. I can sit like a statue on the sofa for long stretches, drooling and saying something like "It can't be done." At these times an outside party usually has to intervene and say, "It's okay. Just do one thing."

Ideally, no outside party would be needed. Ideally, I would tell myself: It's okay. Just do one thing. And once in a while I can. I'm learning to self-soothe.

I'd never heard the term "self-soothe" until my second daughter was born. In the hospital, one of the nurses—pointing to little Jessica peacefully asleep but still moving her lips in a rhythmic mimicry of breast-feeding—remarked, "That baby sure knows how to calm herself down."

When I heard this, a few thoughts occurred to me in a jumbled flash:

1. Good! An "easy" baby!
2. My hours-old baby has skills I don't have.
3. She was born with this? This calming-herself-down thing?

Not long after this, I heard the term "self-soothe" batted about in parenting circles as in "How can I teach my baby to self-soothe so I don't have to get up a thousand times a night?" And when I heard this, more thoughts came, including:

1. It can be taught?
2. Oh, so *that's* what's wrong with me.

All my life I've had trouble talking myself down from a panic. And that's become one of my principal jobs as a writer: learning to take a breath and quietly get back to paddling.

#4: *This Time, Words Will Fail*

This demon is a sort of fear of aphasia: fear that I'll try to write something and no words will come or the words that will come will not be the ones I want. I won't be able to say what I want to say. I'll be reduced to rudimentary grunting.

Writing seems to breed a nagging fear of falling short of the mark. Hence the common sentiment "I don't like writing. I like having written." Anne Lamott's *Bird by Bird* has given so many of us permission to write what she humorously calls "the shitty first draft," the inevitable mediocre version of a piece that must come before there can ever be the hope of a good draft because, as Lamott so eloquently points out, "Very few writers really know what they are doing until they've done it." No matter how long you've been writing, you will be groping in the dark through those bad first drafts, as you try to discover what it is you're trying to say.

And it is truly hideous to have to witness our own grasping and groping. But that's what we writers have to do—bear witness to our inadequacies, our own slow-coming ability to articulate our experiences, our anxiety that this time words will fail us.

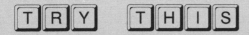

1. Make a list of your own writing demons.

2. Pick one of your demons and give it a name. Write about it for ten minutes.

3. Write for ten minutes on this line from Virginia Valian's essay "Learning to Work": "I also had to learn that losing myself in my work was not dangerous."

4. Write for ten minutes on this: How have you talked yourself out of a panic? How do you self-soothe?

5. When I've told my students about my fear of being "buried alive in the tomb of writing," many have nodded with recognition, and once one of them commented that she never has this fear when writing a long e-mail to a good friend. Other students murmured that this was also true for them. Pick a friend you feel really "gets" you and keep her or him in mind as you write for ten minutes about one of your writing demons. What do you want to tell your friend about the demon?

Conclusion

Writing offers promise. At its best, writing comes from the wild place, from the home of the undomesticated, the untamed, the feral. The place that promises that we *can* bend time and space, the place beyond practicality, punctuality, and iPhones. The place where the force through the green fuse drives the flower, the intersection just before the Summer of Love turns into Altamont. The first sip of the lightly shaken cocktail. The morning of promise before the weariness of the hot afternoon. The foamy strip where the crazy Pacific meets California's flank. The spot where the cable car crests the hill. The moment you first turn the key to the apartment with the heartbreaking hardwoods and the view of the frothy eucalyptus tops that snake through Golden Gate Park.

That's what I'm still hoping for—to shoot past reasonable, to shoot the moon, to risk it all and win, to go beyond routine, obligation, and obedience.

All this makes me sound like the last person you'd want to be in a carpool with.

The truth is, though, most of the time I've shown up for most of what was expected of me. I might not have been PTA president, but just like most everyone I know, I've wheeled the recycling to the curb on Sunday night; I've filled out more permission slips than would seem humanly possible; I've opened the building at eight and locked it up at five; I've replied and RSVPed. Just like you.

And just like most of us, I've yearned for more, to make meaning out of chaos—yes, of course—but more often to make chaos out of far too much order. To remember that the moon is *the moon*, that stars can shoot, and that love can change the course of a day, your night, your life.

And so I write. I write because sometimes—not all the time—when I write, the world recedes just enough for me to see it at a distance, to see that, yes, it does shimmer at dusk and, yes, the story I've made in my mind about how two or three things really are connected—that Frank McCourt reminded me of my dad, that my aunt Pat was teaching me about writing when she leapt ahead of me rock to rock—that these stories mean something, that they count, and that they're as real as the phone bill that needs paying.

Writing offers me relief from my hungry, obsessive mind that wants to run through the same mazes over and over again. Given nothing else to chew on, my mind will obsess on the people in my life, what they're doing, what they could be doing, even—dangerously—what they should be doing. It's not great for relationships, I'll tell you that. Pen in hand, I am often calmed by writing's insistence that I focus on what's in front of me one sentence at a time. The world outside of me starts to blur and then fade and then I'm in this buffered world, something like the hushed world of the deep-sea diver: the visual world bright with fish but the auditory one reduced to just the calming sound of the in and out of breath.

But even if I'm not writing, my mind is often nudging at my work, distracted by it, just as an alcoholic's mind moves to drink. I could easily run a red light parsing through the phrasing of a paragraph in my head. People can be talking to me—my own children—and I might not hear them. It's very possible that my daughters experience my distraction in a way very similar to how I experienced my mother's perennial nap or cocktail hour: She's there but not there. The mother forever just out of reach—but almost imperceptibly so, the remove so subtle that you're likely to blame yourself for not feeling more sure of her presence, her love for you, her purchase on the planet.

The other day I was sitting at a stoplight, my brain rehearsing something I wanted to write. And for a split second I saw myself: a middle-aged woman waiting for the light to change in a quiet neighborhood in Seattle. And I thought: What if the writing, the stories, were suddenly taken away? What if I were sitting here *just* waiting for the light to change? And then *just* turning left, *just* heading home to boil water, rinse lettuce, unload the dishwasher. How empty would life be? How ordinary, how lonely? And then, this enormous wave of gratitude washed over me. Gratitude for having gone down this path, for having this access to magic, this way of remembering that stories count, memories matter, and that the moon is really *the moon*.

Acknowledgments

I'm very grateful to the early readers of this book who cheered me on and propped me up as needed. Sara Kenney, thank you for liking this book from its start and for chiming in later with more love. Sarah C. Harwell, thanks for your insightful readings and support all along the way. I felt like I was writing the book for you two Sara(h)s! Good thing I took that waitressing job at the Lone Wolf Café way back when! Candace Walsh, my writing sister, thanks for getting me and my writing, and thanks to you and your lovely Laura for opening your home to me as a writing retreat. I can still smell the sage and hear the dogs insisting at the screen door. Thanks too for telling me, "Do it, put it all in there. Everything. You can always take it out later." Kathryn Kefauver Goldberg, you're awesome, funny, and talented. Thanks for all your encouragement.

Rachel Klayman: Thank you for your friendship, for teaching me so much about the business of books, and believing in the idea of this book early on.

Philip Patrick: Thanks for saying in the Random House elevator, "I read your blog!"

Radha Marcum, Thomas Mihalik, and Paul Boardman, thanks for reading bits of the book and encouraging me. Thanks to all my writer friends and allies for various forms of support now and back in the day: Doug Schnitzspahn, Andy Gottlieb, Jenny Fan, Mike Medberry, Gretchen Rubin, Jen Singer, Alisa Bowman, Tsh Oxenreider, Jennifer Margulis, Gretchen Roberts, Hope Edelman, Meagan Francis, Kate Hanley, Suzanne Finnamore Luckenbach, John Elder Robison, Jennifer Niesslein, Margot Kahn, David Shields, Cheryl Strayed, E.J. Levy, the Wild Mountain Memoir Retreat staff, and all the writers who came to Wild Mountain.

Roxanne Ray, Kathy Eisele, Sarah Naughton, and Lori Polemenakos, thanks for giving me so much bill-paying work to support my book-writing habit.

All my memoir students at the University of Washington: Thank you for listening to my "how I found my voice" stories and for your dedication to the craft of writing.

Carlene Cross: I love sharing the ups and downs of writing and life with you.

Nicole Aloni: Thanks for your friendship, great ideas, and your boundless optimism.

Natalie Singer: I'm so happy you're my friend!

Paula Temple, aka Hun: You are *such* a good friend to me. Thank you for expecting the best for me.

Anika Nelson Bavas: Since we became friends in the MFA

program sixteen years ago, our lives have gone through a dozen incarnations, but your loyalty is constant. Thanks for being such an amazing friend.

Many thanks to Anjali Singh and Millicent Bennett for all the dedication, wisdom, and intelligence that you both brought to the editing process. I appreciate your insights so much. I'm also grateful to Michele Bové, Sarah Nalle, and all the other folks at Simon & Schuster for their relentless efforts.

Elisabeth Weed, you're my dream agent. You talk to me on the phone! You watch out for me! You sold this crazy book! Thank you so much!

My mom: I appreciate all your support. No one wants their child to grow up and write about them. Thanks for understanding!

And most of all: My kids. You guys are the best! I'm so proud of both of you. It's not easy to have a mom who works at home, always hovering around but yet never really fully available. But yet you deal with it. I'm the luckiest mom in the world. I love you!

Recommended Reading

Interested in learning more about personal narrative and memoir as a genre? Here are some books you might want to read:

Barrington, Judith. *Writing the Memoir: From Truth to Art*. Portland, OR: Eighth Mountain Press, 2002.

Goldberg, Natalie. *Old Friend from Far Away: The Practice of Writing Memoir*. New York: Free Press, 2007.

Gornick, Vivian. *The Situation and the Story: The Art of Personal Narrative*. New York: Farrar, Straus and Giroux, 2002.

Hampl, Patricia. *I Could Tell You Stories: Sojourns in the Land of Memory*. New York: W. W. Norton, 2000.

Lopate, Phillip. *To Show and To Tell: The Craft of Literary Nonfiction*. New York: Free Press, 2013.

———, ed. *The Art of the Personal Essay: An Anthology from the Classical Era to the Present*. New York: Anchor, 1997. If nothing else, read Lopate's introduction, a beautifully written and thorough examination of the essay form.

Norton, Lisa Dale. *Shimmering Images: A Handy Little Guide to Writing Memoir*. New York: St. Martin's Griffin, 2008.

Rainer, Tristine. *Your Life as Story: Discovering the "New Autobiography" and Writing Memoir as Literature*. New York: Tarcher, 1998.

Shields, David. *Reality Hunger: A Manifesto*. New York: Vintage, 2011.

Silverman, Sue William. *Fearless Confessions: A Writer's Guide to Memoir*. Athens: University of Georgia Press, 2009.

Some encouraging books that might help you when you feel stuck:

Cameron, Julia. *How To Avoid Making Art (or Anything Else You Enjoy)*. New York: Tarcher, 2005.

———. *The Right to Write: An Invitation and Initiation into the Writing Life*. New York: Tarcher, 1998.

Dillard, Annie. *The Writing Life*. New York: HarperPerennial, 1990.

Goldberg, Natalie. *Writing Down the Bones: Freeing the Writer Within*. New York: Shambhala, 1986.

Lamott, Anne. *Bird by Bird: Some Instructions on Writing and Life*. New York: Anchor, 1995.

Strayed, Cheryl. *Tiny Beautiful Things: Advice on Love and Life from Dear Sugar*. New York: Vintage, 2012.

Tharp, Twyla. *The Creative Habit: Learn It and Use It for Life*. New York: Simon & Schuster, 2003.

Valian, Virginia. "Learning to Work." Full text of this essay available at http://writingismydrink.com/learning-to-work/.

About the Author

Theo Pauline Nestor is the author of *How to Sleep Alone in a King-Size Bed: A Memoir of Starting Over* (Crown, 2008), which was selected by *Kirkus Reviews* as a "2008 Top Pick for Reading Groups" and by Target as a "Breakout Book." Her work has been published in numerous places including the *New York Times*, the Huffington Post, *Alligator Juniper*, and *Brain, Child* magazine. An award-winning instructor, Nestor is the instructor for the University of Washington's Professional & Continuing Education department's Certificate in Memoir and a founder of the Wild Mountain Memoir Retreat. She lives in Seattle with her family and cat. You can find her blog at WritingIsMyDrink.com.